The **Mungaka**
Alphabet Workbook

The Mungaka Alphabet Workbook

Dù'ti mà Fuŋ boà mà Ŋwà'ni Mìŋgâkà

Jude Fokwang & Godlove Gwaabe

Second Edition

SPEARS BOOKS

Denver, Colorado

Spears Books
An Imprint of Spears Media Press LLC
21699 E. Quincy Ave, Unit F #167
Aurora, CO 80015
United States of America

First published in the United States of America in 2020 by Spears Books
Second edition published in 2026 by Spears Books
www.spearsbooks.org
info@spearsmedia.com
Information on this title: www.spearsbooks.org/the-mungaka-alphabet-workbook-2nd-edition
© 2026 Jude Fokwang & Godlove Gwaabe
All rights reserved.

ISBN: 9781957296630 (Paperback)

Design and typesetting by Spears Media Press LLC, Denver, CO

To all our basic learners who have persevered throughout the years in their determination to learn how to read, write and speak Mungaka.

Contents

Section Three: Consonants

PREFACE TO THE SECOND EDITION

It has been slightly over five years since the first edition of the *Mungaka Alphabet Workbook* was released during the COVID-19 pandemic. We had hoped to publish a second edition within two or three years of the first release, but for many reasons, that did not materialize. However, soon after the first edition's publication, we effectively used it as a primer for teaching *Mungaka 201*, a course designed exclusively for native speakers. Our users found the workbook both useful and effective, but they also noted that the exercises at the end of each lesson lacked answers. Without an answer key, there was no way for learners to assess their performance without instructor feedback. We are therefore pleased to share that this edition includes a comprehensive answer key to all the exercises, which we hope will make learning even more effective.

In addition to the answer key, we have corrected several tonal and spelling errors that appeared in the first edition. The layout has also been improved with the inclusion of a notes section at the end of most chapters. We hope users will use these spaces to jot down any challenges, words, or sentences inspired by each lesson. We remain readily available to receive feedback and ensure that learners get the most out of this workbook.

Finally, we wish to clarify that this workbook will be most useful to native speakers, although it does include elements suitable for beginners. Learners are expected to have some pre-existing knowledge of Mungaka and to draw on their growing mastery of vocabulary when responding to prompts and exercises. Beginners will find it particularly helpful for learning new words and understanding the structure of Mungaka sentences, as translations are provided for all the exercises. The "matching pairs" activity at the end of the workbook is designed for beginners and tests their knowledge of basic Mungaka vocabulary. We also strongly encourage learners to practice sounding out the words in lessons that require oral repetition. For a tonal language such as Mungaka, it is not enough to sound them out silently in your mind.

We hope this second edition will add value to your learning and help you grow in confidence in your ability to read and write Mungaka.

Jude Fokwang
August 19, 2025
Denver, Colorado

PREFACE TO THE FIRST EDITION

When I published *The New Mungaka Alphabet for Beginners* in 2017, the next vision was to help both adult and elementary school learners master the essence of the new standardized alphabet. I know many individuals who had complained about the complexity of the old alphabet (adapted from the German alphabet) and were very enthusiastic about the simplicity of the new alphabet. Although the introduction of the new alphabet was a much welcome change, we soon realized that it would take considerable effort to learn how to write some of the letters not found on a standard keyboard, but also that mastering the tones would take even more committed effort.

We knew there was a curriculum being run out of Bali, but it was not easy to lay hands on instructional materials. I soon realized that I would either have to wait for an eternity for these materials or begin to develop something for my children, other young learners and of course, adult native speakers interested in becoming literate in Mungaka. Given the technological resources at our disposal, it was just a matter of time before this vision would become a reality. I was familiar with the Zoom platform from my teaching work and found it a perfect fit for our prospective course. But this would not be sufficient to launch the vision of a Mungaka 101 online course. I needed content and possibly, a co-instructor familiar with the New Mungaka Alphabet. Ni Goddy Gwaabe generously accepted my offer to join me as co-instructor for Mungaka 101. It became clear soon after our initial interaction that he had completed a course on the new Mungaka alphabet in Bali and had a teaching background. These qualities would be of tremendous help in our preparation to roll out Mungaka 101. Needless to add that he and I have learned a great deal during these past years as we continue to comb through every resource we can find in order to provide a stimulating and enjoyable experience for our learners.

In the fall of 2018, we launched the first ever course in the Bali diaspora dedicated to the teaching of Mungaka. Our initial cohort included young learners from Canada and the USA. The course ran for fourteen weeks (September through December) – a structure that has become standardized. We used the Zoom platform, taking advantage of the free 40 minutes it provided to non-subscribed users. After the initial 40 minutes had expired, we would re-launch and continue with our lessons. The first half of the class was generally devoted to basic sound practice and the second half to reading and writing. Our learners were enthusiastic, determined and hardworking. We tried our best to make the classes fun, interactive and productive. Many looked forward to our Sunday classes and overtime,

Sundays during the academic year had become synonymous with Mungaka online classes. At the end of our first academic year, two certificates were issued to two of our most dedicated learners. Our vision had finally paid off, especially as the second semester (spring 2019) saw the enrolment of several adult learners.

Although *The New Mungaka Alphabet for Beginners* served as the required text for our course, we soon realized that it was far from being a suitable course material. Humbled by this recognition, we decided to beef up the content we had developed over the course of two years into a workbook format. Thus, what you have in your hands is the product of over two years of dedicated engagement with the most basic elements of Mungaka. You will also find new features and additions which, hopefully, will simplify your learning. It is our hope that between these pages, you will find a very essential and productive companion to your dream of learning Mungaka. Our aim is to present you with the basics of what it takes to read and write Mungaka. This book will not help you become a fluent speaker of Mungaka, but it provides the basis upon which your interest may be further developed and nurtured into maturity.

If you are a first-time learner, we are glad to count you amongst our rank. If you are a returning learner, we thank you for your continued interest in becoming literate in Mungaka and we look forward to many fruitful years of learning, writing, reading and above all, speaking Mungaka.

Jude Fokwang
Course Director, Mungaka 101

ACKNOWLEDGEMENTS

This book is the outcome of several years of experimentation with teaching an online language course. Despite the opportunities afforded by an online platform, we have also faced challenges. However, our spirits and devotion have been bolstered by a band of joyous cheerleaders who have not relented in cheering us on. We remain grateful to the first batch of students who enthusiastically enrolled in Mungaka 101 and trod along with us, despite the uncertainty of how our first semester would turn out. Our adult learners have continued to engage and inspire us in more ways than can be outlined: Ni Fidelis Kaspa brought exceptional zeal and a deep knowledge of spoken Mungaka to our lessons. He hardly missed a class even when he had to work on Sundays – sometimes while he drove to work or during his breaktime. Ni Fidelis Kaspa became one of our most ardent ambassadors and didn't fail to tell everyone within his social circle how important it was for them to become literate in Mungaka. Other adult learners like Ma Irene Tita and Ma Besona Sikod continue to teach us that true dedication yields fruits. They have gone above and beyond in their commitment to learn the essentials of written and spoken Mungaka. Ma Irene contributed to the sounds of the Kindle edition of the alphabet book and has provided feedback that we have found deeply rewarding. Ma Muyo Galega and her daughter, Ma Kenna Galega were amongst the first cohort of students in Mungaka101 and their joint engagements in the course demonstrated a rare commitment and determination. They both fulfilled the course expectations and were amongst our first recipients of a course completion certificate. To them, we say congratulations and a huge thanks. Tita Nyugha Galega joined us during the second offering of the course in the spring of 2019 and has remained a devoted student and ambassador of Mungaka 101. His advocacy in getting a critical mass that can read, write and speak Mungaka is deeply appreciated. One of those who also joined our Mungaka literacy campaign on day one was Ma Lilian Fokwang. She has continued to entertain us with her witty short stories, intriguing sentences and overall promotion of Mungaka in the Bali Cultural Association newsletter. Ma Lynn Cockburn also joined us on day one. Ma Lynn has challenged herself over the years, consistently adding new Mungaka vocabulary to her repertoire and demonstrates in word and deed that she loves Bali and her people. Ma Lynn has advocated the translation of useful health information into Mungaka and always brings unique insights about preparing didactic materials for a young audience.

We wish to acknowledge other basic adult learners who have joined and contributed significantly to the growth of our Mungaka 101 community: Ma Evelyn Nahjelah Commerford, Ma Comfort Sema, Ma Alice Lima, Ni Dema Govalla, Ni Walla Govalla, Ba Joe Fomukong, Ma Kah Fomukong and Ni Eric Titabandong. Ma Lilian Fomunung and Ba Nkom Gwanbidpua Tangeh have been consistent in their encouragement of our vision. We look forward to them joining our class sessions as we promote Mungaka literacy in the Bali diaspora.

Ba Nkom Gwannua Ndangam, a seasoned linguist and teacher has provided more than just encouragement to our initiative. He attended a few sessions, guest-lectured and supported us with additional instructional materials, some of which we hope to incorporate in future editions of this workbook. We couldn't be more grateful for Ba Nkom Gwannua's support.

Finally, our gratitude goes to the Culture Committee chair of the Bali Cultural Association (USA), Ni Samkeah Titanji, who upon learning about our initiative, advocated for the deployment of BCA-USA resources to support our learners. Thanks to the committee, we have been able to afford a paid subscription for BookWidgets and Zoom Video, resources that have significantly contributed to the ease of our students' learning. BookWidgets is an online platform that allows teachers to develop multiple types of instructional materials from flashcards with sound to quizzes and games.

A workbook of this length and variety of themes and exercises is far from perfect. We encourage constructive feedback on how future editions of this remarkable effort may be improved. We recognize as well that we as the instructors are first and foremost, devoted learners and that our efforts are not error-free. Consequently, any deficiencies found in this workbook are entirely ours and should not be attributed to anyone else.

The MUNGAKA
ALPHABET
WORKBOOK

INTRODUCTION

This workbook synthesizes materials we have developed since the initiation of an online course known as Mungaka 101 in 2018. It is intended to provide users with a deeper understanding of the new Mungaka alphabet, its sounds and other basic writing conventions. Although it is prepared with a Mungaka 101 learner in mind, the book could be useful for individuals who have never taken a course in the new alphabet. We have therefore aimed to provide the reader with a broad but elementary material that will enable them to master the essentials of the Mungaka alphabet and how to use them in everyday written and spoken contexts.

A considerable amount of information has been written about the origins of Mungaka (V. Titanji, Gwanfogbe, Nwana, Ndangam, & Lima, 1988) and its adoption as a language of literacy since the colonial era to the present (Fokwang, 2017; Ndangam, 2014; Tasama, 2016; Tischhauser, 1992; B. K. L. L. Titanji, 2016). These sources are invaluable in learning more about the language's development and linguistic nuances. However, it is important to note here that the new Mungaka alphabet is a significant departure from its German–inspired format, originally developed by Swiss missionaries during the early colonial period. The new alphabet draws from the General Alphabet of Cameroon Languages adopted in 1979 (Tadadjeu & Sadembouo, 1979). This general alphabet serves as a common pool from which each indigenous language community may develop its orthography based on its unique linguistic realities. To this end, Mungaka linguists have adapted and trained native speakers on the new orthography (Tasama, 2016). The alphabet employed in this workbook is consistent with the standardized and simplified new Mungaka alphabet and furthers the magnificent work initiated by Juliette Tasama and her colleagues.

Elementary Grammar in Mungaka

As it stands, there is no authoritative book on Mungaka grammar although Tischhauser & Stöckle's *Mungaka (Bali) Dictionary* (1992) does a tremendous job with outlining some of the essential grammatical principles. In this book, we focus on three common grammatical categories: pronouns, nouns and verbs.

Pronouns

The Merriam–Webster dictionary defines a pronoun as "any of a small set of words in a language that are used as substitutes for nouns or noun phrases and whose referents are named or understood in the context." Examples of pronouns in Mungaka include the following:

Mungaka Pronoun	English Equivalent
i, ì	He/she/it
u, ù	You
a, à	My, it

These pronouns and more shall be examined in detail as they occur, especially when a sound or letter serves as a standalone word.

Nouns

The Merriam–Webster dictionary defines a noun as "any member of a class of words that typically can be combined with determiners to serve as the subject of a verb, can be interpreted as singular or plural, can be replaced with a pronoun, and refer to an entity, quality, state, action, or concept." Each chapter concludes with a glossary of words which we have categorized into nouns and verbs and occasionally, an adverb or adjective is added. Examples of nouns in Mungaka include: ŋwà'nì (book), nchì (water), bòn (people) etc.

Verbs

The Merriam–Webster dictionary defines a verb as "a word that characteristically is the grammatical center of a predicate and expresses an act, occurrence, or mode of being, that in various languages is inflected for agreement with the subject, for tense, for voice, for mood, or for aspect, and that typically has rather full descriptive meaning and characterizing quality ..."

When they occur in their infinitive form, verbs in Mungaka are often denoted by the prefix (**mà**) followed by the word; e.g. **mà jǐd** (to walk), **mà jɨ** (to eat). You will notice that this prefix is omitted in the chapter glossary as a matter of convention. Many Mungaka verbs can be easily identified by their suffixes – i.e. by the nature of the way the words end. Some common suffixes include: **–ni, –'ni, –'ti, –li, –ti**. Examples of such verbs include: **mà jɨ'ti** (to feed), **mà nèbti** (to fix, repair), **mà kɜ̀li** (to hang something). For details about this grammatical feature, we refer you to Stöckle's dictionary.

In this workbook, learners are invited to identify nouns and verbs. It is intended that these exercises will enable you to become proficient in breaking down Mungaka speech forms into their component parts – a practice that will hopefully improve your writing significantly. Future editions of the workbook will extend the exercises to other grammatical categories such as adverbs and adjectives.

Typing in Mungaka

What good would it serve if we learned how to read Mungaka but are unable to write it? This reader aims to achieve two things: help the learner to read and write Mungaka following the prevailing linguistic conventions. Basic learners may begin with writing in a notebook using a pen or pencil. However, we are endowed with many electronic options which we will cover below.

Keyman

It is easy to type Mungaka using the Keyman keyboard. The following additional information is culled from the Keyman website (keyman.com/about).

> Originally created in 1993 to type Lao on Windows, Keyman is now a free and open source keyboarding platform which allows anyone to write a keyboard layout for their language. Keyman is available for many platforms, including Windows, macOS, iOS, Android, Linux and the web.
>
> Keyboard layouts are defined with a clear and easy to understand keyboard grammar. Keyman's contextual input model means keyboard layouts can be intelligent and make it simple to type even the most complex languages. Keyboard layouts are distributed through an open catalog to all major desktop and mobile platforms."
>
> Keyman is created by SIL International. Partners in Language Development, SIL International is a faith–based nonprofit organization committed to serving language communities worldwide as they build capacity for sustainable language development. SIL does this primarily through research, translation, training and materials development.

As stated above, Keyman is open source and available on all electronic platforms including personal computers and mobile phones. For a start, you will need to download a single package of the Keyman application, available for both Mac OS and Windows PC. The software is currently in version 13 and enjoys frequent updates. PC users are encouraged to download the software by following this link: https://keyman.com/keyboards/cameroonqwertyunicode50 and to follow the instructions to complete the installation. Mac users are encouraged to visit the Keyman website for additional installation instructions.

The keyboard supports all Cameroon languages with a single, standardized layout based on the US English keyboard. Once you have downloaded and installed the Keyman Desktop, proceed to download the Cameroon language of your choice, in this case, Mungaka. This can be easily done from within the application. One final task is to install suitable font types that would display the alphabet correctly. Download and install any of the following fonts: Charis SIL or Doulos SIL and you are ready to start typing. The Cambria font which comes installed on most computers is also equipped to render the Mungaka alphabet.

The next challenge addresses the issue of how to type the appropriate keyboard combinations to produce non-English letters (e.g. ɨ, ə or tones such as ǎ, â etc). The Keyman website provides an outline of the keyboard combinations that will assist you in writing these letters. The keyboard is reproduced below for your convenience.

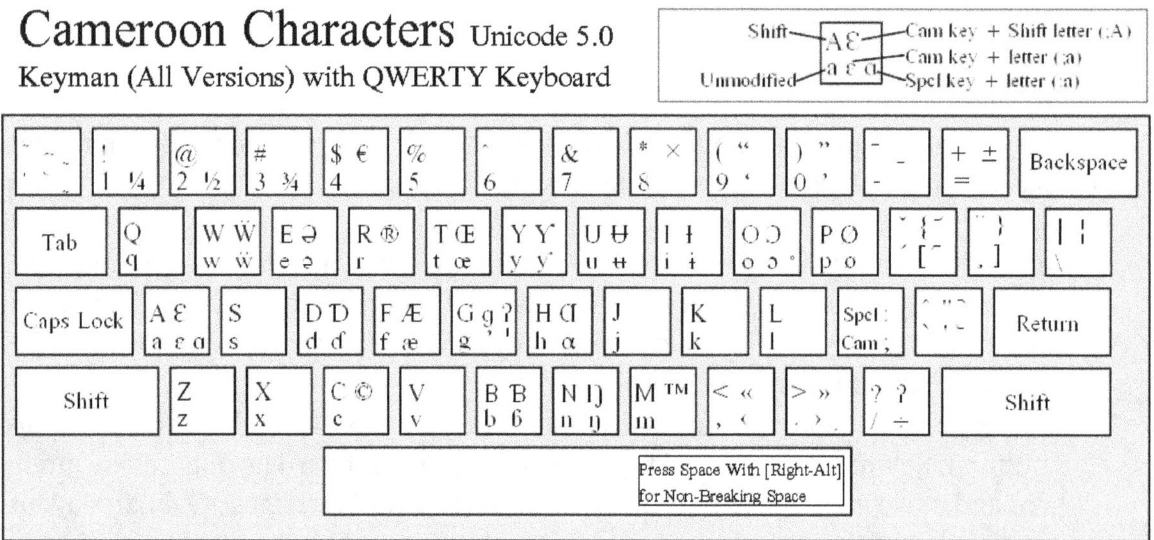

We recommend that you have a printout of the Cameroon Characters Keyboard, positioned in an area where you may easily cross-check the combinations as you type. The first couple of attempts may seem challenging but as you practice more, you will become efficient in typing the key combinations.

Keyman is also available for mobile devices. Unlike the desktop process, you will find the mobile interfaces even easier to navigate and use.

SwiftKey

SwiftKey is an alternative mobile device keyboard originally developed by TouchType and later acquired by Microsoft. The iOS version is somehow limited but Swiftkey in Android allows the user to type in up to five different languages. Although Mungaka is not listed as one of the supported languages, there are two Ngemba languages which when activated, allow the user to type all Mungaka characters without leaving the keyboard interface. Should you opt to install SwiftKey, proceed to activate the following languages (Bafut and Ngemba). Hopefully, Microsoft will include Mungaka in future as a standalone language.

The reader may wish to know the main difference between Keyman and SwiftKey. Keyman has a separate app and a note-taking area where writers may compose their text, after which you will have to copy and paste the composed text in a new application.

This could be cumbersome especially if you wished to write just a single sentence or so. SwiftKey on the other hand permits the user to type the letters with their diacritics (tonal indicators) already embedded in the letters. This permits the writer to use the keyboard in any application with the same QWERTY layout we are accustomed to. Keyman's layout on the other hand leaves the writer to inscribe the tones as they see fit. An added advantage with SwiftKey is that it remembers your writing style and spelling by means of artificial intelligence. Over time, this would make typing certain words predictable and faster.

How to input Mungaka characters on Keyman for Desktop

Character	Type	Diacritic	Graph	Type
ɛ	;a	Low	`	'
Ɛ	;a	High	´	[
ə	;e	Falling	^	"
Ə	;e	Rising	ˇ	{
ɨ	;i	Glottal stop	'	;g
Ɨ	;i			
ŋ	;n			
Ŋ	;n			
ɔ	;o			
Ɔ	;o			

For users with sufficient space on their phones, it may help to have both applications installed. You may choose to switch between them depending on your needs. For extended typing projects, we recommend you have Keyman for desktop which has proven to be a very dependable resource over the years. Once you overcome the initial learning phase, typing Mungaka should be fun and a very rewarding experience.

How to use this workbook

This book is divided into three main sections. The first section introduces the student to the basics of Mungaka tones and vowels. Each item is accompanied by brief exercises where the user is expected to engage with the learnt material.

Section two is devoted to Mungaka vowels. As you will find out shortly, Mungaka has more vowels than the English language. Writing some of these vowels requires the installation of the keyboards mentioned in the previous section of this introduction. Each vowel is introduced with an exercise on sound practice that enables the learner to master the distinct sound produced by the letter. Here, the focus is just on the sounds and their tones. The meanings of these words are provided at the end of each chapter in the glossary section. The learner is further invited to identify various components of speech such as nouns and verbs. This same pattern is employed in the third section devoted to consonants. It is our hope that this workbook will engage the new or returning learner in multiple ways. It provides extensive room to practice one's writing by testing your mastery of tones, spelling and overall vocabulary. We hope the choice of this book puts you in the right path towards proficiency in Mungaka.

Bibliography

Fokwang, J. (2017). *The New Mungaka Alphabet for Beginners*. Denver, Colorado: Spears Media Press.

Ndangam, G. (2014). *Cultural Encounters: Society, Culture and Language in Bali Nyonga From the 19th Century*. Collierville, TN: Instantpublisher.com.

Tadadjeu, M., & Sadembouo, E. (1979). *Alphabet général des langues camerounaises / General Alphabet of Cameroon Languages*. Retrieved from Département des Langues Africaines et Linguistique, Faculté des Lettres et Sciences Humaines (F.L.S.H), Université de Yaoundé:

Tasama, J. N. (2016). The Rehabilitation and Revival of Mungaka for Literacy. In V. P. K. Titanji (Ed.), *Bali Nyonga Today: Roots, Cultural Practices and Future Perspectives* (pp. 114–136). Denver, Colorado: Spears Media Press.

Tischhauser, G. (1992). *Mungaka (Bali) Dictionary* (J. Stöckle, Trans. Vol. Vol. 1). Cologne: Rüdiger Köppe Publishers.

Titanji, B. K. L. L. (2016). Mungaka in Perspective: Past, Present and Future Trends. In V. P. K. Titanji (Ed.), *Bali Nyonga Today: Roots, Cultural Practices and Future Perspectives* (pp. 137–146). Denver, Colorado: Spears Media Press.

Titanji, V., Gwanfogbe, M., Nwana, E. M., Ndangam, A. F., & Lima, A. S. (Eds.). (1988). *An Introduction to the Study of Bali-Nyonga (A tribute to His Royal Highness Galega II, Traditional Ruler of Bali-Nyonga from 1940–1985)*. Yaoundé: Stardust Printers.

SECTION ONE

Tones and Vowels

THE MUNGAKA ALPHABET

Uppercase	Lowercase		Uppercase	Lowercase
A	a		K	k
B	b		L	l
CH	ch		M	m
D	d		N	n
E	e		NY	ny
Ɛ	ɛ		Ŋ	ŋ
Ə	ə		O	o
F	f		Ɔ	ɔ
G	g		P	p
GH	gh		S	s
H	h		T	t
I	i		U	u
Ɨ	ɨ		V	v
J	j		W	w
			Y	y

CHAPTER 1

TONES IN MUNGAKA

Mungaka is a tonal language. Most languages in the world are tonal. When we say a language is tonal, it means that a change in pitch (sound) in a word with similar spelling results in a change in the meaning of the word. The tones are marked by different diacritics and this is essential to master any tonal language.

How Many Tones are there in Mungaka?

Some linguists have suggested that Mungaka has **five** (5) tones although one of them (mid tone) occurs infrequently. For the purpose of this workbook, we shall limit ourselves to **four tones**: high, low, rising, and falling tones. You should remember this as a general principle that tones in Mungaka are only indicated on vowels.

Lesson 1A: High Tone

The high tone is normally indicated by the ***acute accent*** as in [á]. However, this is not marked in Mungaka.

Examples of words with high tone are: **taŋ, ta, ba, ma, ni, mon, ndab, tab** etc.

Write down three new words with high tone in the space below:

....

....

....

....

Lesson 1B: Low Tone

The low tone is marked in Mungaka by a grave accent as in [à].

Examples of words with low tone are: **bòn, tà, bà, bàm, tàŋ** etc.

Can you think of three new words with low tones?

....

....

....

....

Lesson 1C: Rising Tone

The rising tone means that the pitch begins low and ends high. It is marked in Mungaka with a "hacek" as in [ǎ] which combines the low tone mark grave accent followed by the high tone acute accent. There are a few principles that guide the use of the rising tone in Mungaka.

First, there is a class of nouns and verbs that simply carry the rising tone; for these words, you will simply have to learn them as you improve your vocabulary in Mungaka.
Examples of words in Mungaka that have the rising tone are: **lǎ, fǔb, tǎ, lǎb, fǒd** etc.

Can you think of three new words that regularly carry a rising tone?

....

....

....

....

Next, keep in mind that there are a class of compound nouns which normally have low tones, but when these nouns are followed by nouns with high tones, the former are transformed into rising tones.

Some examples include the following:

Low tone noun	High tone noun	Applied Rising Tone
Bɔ̀m	ŋgab	Bɔ̌m ŋgab
Kù	ŋgab	Kǔ ŋgab
Nchì	chaŋ	nchǐ chaŋ

Write down three nouns that normally have low tones but get transformed when followed by another noun with high tone?

....
....
....
....

Finally, there are a class of compound nouns which normally have low tones, but when these nouns are followed by nouns with low tones, the former are transformed into rising tones.

Consider the examples below:

Low tone noun	Low tone noun	Applied Rising Tone
Bɔ̀m	mɨ̀n	Bɔ̌m mɨ̀n
Kù	mbàb	Kǔ mbàb
Lèŋ	Tìtà	Lěŋ Tìtà

Write down three nouns that normally have low tones but get transformed when followed by another noun with high tone?

....
....
....
....

Lesson 1D: Falling Tones

The falling tone is traditionally marked with a circumflex [â]. This means that the tone starts high (acute accent) and ends low (grave accent). There are three principles that guide the use of the falling tone in Mungaka.

1) All compound nouns that are prefixed by the root, **mon** tend to have the falling tone. The prefix *mon* (child) denotes – items that are **small** or simply **some**. You'll also notice that the (–n) is deleted from the compound noun.

Some examples of words that conform to the above principle are:
Mômbɔd – baby
Môkun – small bed
mômfa' – twin
Môkaŋ – small bowl, or plate

Write down two words that have the prefix –mô:

....

....

....

....

2) All compound nouns that are prefixed by the root **mâ** tend to have the falling tone. The prefix **mâ** (mother) denotes the qualities of *big, great, important.*

Some examples of words that conform to this principle are:
    Mâmbi – mother goat
    Mâŋgɔb – mother hen
    Mânù – important matter, thing
    Mândab – big or massive house

Write down two or three words that have the prefix – mâ:

....

....

....

....

3) In the last principle, all stems of noun classes that have high tones followed by low tone nouns are transformed into falling tones. Let us look at a few examples:
- Ndɔŋ – is normally high–tone. However, when it is followed by a noun with a low tone (e.g. mfɔ̀ŋ), it then becomes **ndɔ̂ŋ mfɔ̀ŋ**.
- Mon normally has a high tone but when followed by the word (mfòn – king), it becomes **mô mfòn.**
- Ntu' (cup) has a high tone, but when followed by the word tìtà (prince, captain), then it becomes – **ntû' tìtà** (the prince's cup).

Write down two sentences below that demonstrate your understanding of the above principle:

....

....

....

....

SECTION TWO

Vowels

NOTES

CHAPTER 2

VOWELS IN MUNGAKA

Vowels are a class of speech sounds made with the vocal tract open. Unlike the English language that has five (5) vowels (a, e, i, o, u – sometimes y) Mungaka has nine (9) standard vowels: a, e, ɛ, ə, i, ɨ, o, ɔ, u. If we add the different tones to these sounds, then Mungaka possibly has dozens of vowels. However, to simplify our learning, we'll restrict ourselves to the nine vowels listed above. The four additional non–English vowels will help us to write the sounds in Mungaka as best as we can.

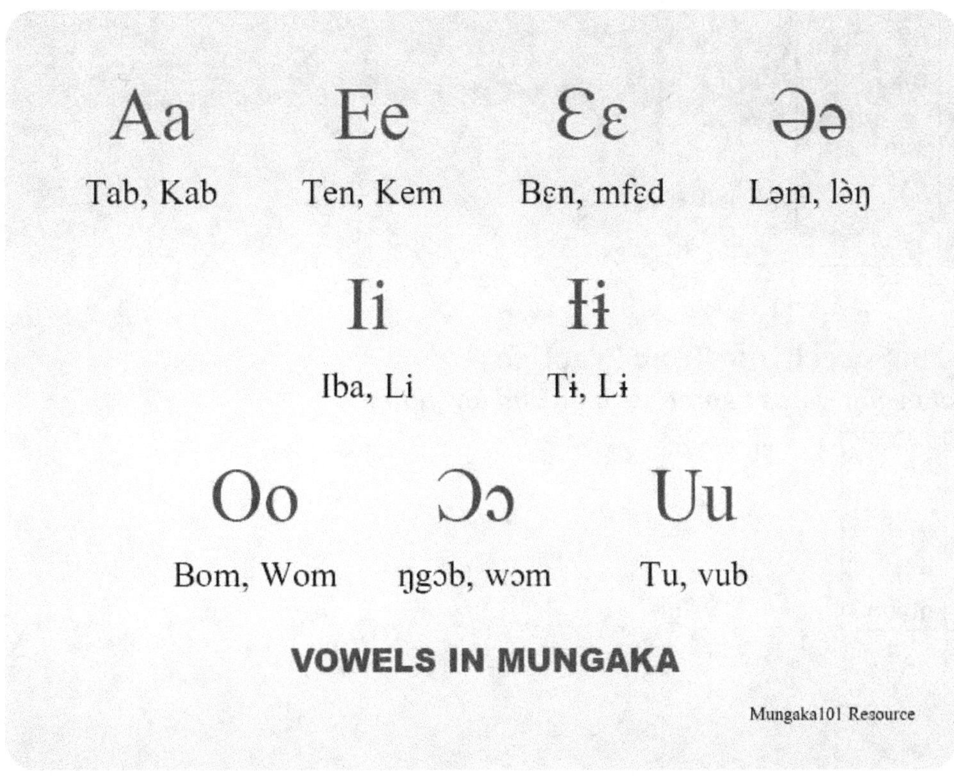

A & E

Letter [a] is sounded as in the English word bat /bæt/. Relatively few words in Mungaka begin with letter [a]. However, letter [a] with different tones has several meanings and grammatical categories which we will examine below.

The letter [e] is pronounced in Mungaka as in the English word bait /beyt/ or ate /et/. Just like letter [a], there few or no common words that begin with letter [e] but you will find this vowel in so many different words.

Lesson 2A: Practice the sounds of speech

Read out the words in the first column, then read the words in the second column; then read the words in pairs contrasting the vowel sounds.

[a]	[e]
Fa	Fĕ
Kǎ	Kĕ
Wà	Wĕ
Mfa	Mfè
Sà	Sĕ
Yǎnù	Yeba

Lesson 2B: Speech and Tone Practice

Say the following words to practice high and low tones.

Kà	Kè
Kan	ŋkèn
Ka	Kà
Mba	mbàŋ

Lesson 2C: Grammar and Vocabulary with [a] Sound

Letter [à] with a low tone may be used as an animate or inanimate pronoun.

1) À lîn wù ndǐn ndab lɛ – it is you who know the house
2) À bê mì ɛ? – how is it?

Letter [à] with a low tone and sometimes with a high tone [a] may be used as a possessive pronoun; kùŋ a – my box; bàm a – my bag

Although very few words begin with letter [a] in Mungaka, the vowel is found in many words. We'll examine a few verbs and nouns that have the vowel [a].

Underline the nouns in the sentences below:

1) Mbàb lɛ majǐ bàm – The mouse is in the bag.
2) Bǎm mon majǐ ndab – The baby's bag is in the house.
3) Ntěd mfŏn ma tu mbad – The king's palace is on a hill.

Underline the verbs in the sentences below:

1) Mbi lɛ nì nlad chi – The goat is licking salt.
2) Bì to bà kab sànjàb – Come let us harvest some vegetables.
3) Fa mì mfam itàn – Give me five nails

Exercise 2D: Grammar and Vocabulary with [e] Sound

Underline the nouns in the sentences below:

1) Mon ma ndùn kè – The baby is on the mat.
2) Nà'sàŋ ja'nî mbìyaŋ ma ndùn kè – Nahsang has dried peanuts on the mat.
3) Bà led jam ma fà' tì – There are lots of ticks on the farm.
4) Led jam ndû yɔ̀ nyàm tì – This animal has a lot of ticks.
5) Nswen kà vî bon ited – The elephant gave birth to three calves.
6) Bì to bà nyî̀ŋ Lela – Come let's celebrate Lela.

Underline the verbs in the sentences below:

1) Ba kà kê' ndab lɛ – Father unlocked the door (literally the house).
2) Bùma nèbti mɨ lə̀ŋ – Buma has made a chair.
3) Bǎm ba lěd tìtì – Father's bag is very heavy.
4) Kè'mia kà běd mà no nchì – Kehmia refused to drink water.

5) Jàla běd mà cho motò – Jala refused to get into the car.

Exercise 2E: Spelling and Tones

Circle the misspelled words or those whose tones have not been properly marked. Then write the correct word in the space provided.

1) Mbab lɛ majǐ bam – The mouse is in the bag.

....

2) Bam nǎ majǐ ndab – Mother's bag is in the house.

....

3) Dɔb boà na nì ŋkaŋ puff puff – Dob and mother are frying puff puff.

....

4) Na lǐn ma naŋ mpà – Mother knows how to cook the mpa soup.

....

5) Mon bed mà li – The child has refused to sleep.

....

6) Nǎ ja'nî mbìyaŋ ma ndùn ke – Mother has dried peanuts on the mat.

....

7) Fa mɨ ke'fɨn ù – Give me your key.

....

8) Kùna we' nji i mfi – Kuna has put on her new dress.

....

Chapter Glossary

	Nouns	Verbs
[a]	Kǎ – grandmother Wà – a type of tree Mfa – necklace Sà – witchcraft Mba – a mad person Mbàŋ – seed, kernel Ndab – house, home Mbàb – house mouse Bàm – bag, sack Mbad – hill Mfam – nail Fà' – farm, garden Nyàm – animal	Fa – to give, donate Kan – to be tired Lad – to lick Kab – to pluck, harvest Ja'ni – to dry out
	Nouns	**Verbs**
[e]	Kè – mat Kě – things (plural) Ŋkèn – gift, donation Mfè – feather Ntèd – palace Nswen – elephant Ited – number 3 Kě'fɨn – key	Wě – to catch Sě – to tear Běd – to deny, refuse Nèbti – to fix, construct, repair Kě' – to open, unlock

NOTES

ɛ & ə

In this chapter, we shall examine two distinctive sounds in Mungaka – namely [ɛ] and [ə]. The letter [ɛ] is sounded in similar fashion as the vowel in the English word, bet /bɛt/. As usual, we shall examine occurrences of this vowel in nouns and verbs in the sentences below.

The letter [ə] is sounded in similar fashion as the vowel in the English word, urban /ər–bən/. We will begin with sound practice to enable you learn how to distinguish these two sounds.

Lesson 3A: Practice the sounds of Speech

Read out the words in the first column, then read the words in the second column; then read the words in pairs contrasting the vowel sounds.

[ɛ]	[ə]
Bɛn	Mbə̀ŋ
Ŋgɛ̀n	Ŋgə̀d
Jɛd	Jə̆
Mɛ̀n	Lə̆m
Kɛn	Kə̀m
Kɛ̀ti	Kə̀li

Exercise 3B: Grammar and Vocabulary with [ɛ] Sound

Underline the nouns in the sentences below:

1) Bon nì nyǐŋ bɛn ma ndab – The kids are dancing in the house
2) Bùma wê ŋgɛ̀n iba – Buma has caught two grasshoppers.
3) Kènna batî yǐ nă ma ŋgwɛn – Kenna has followed her mother to the farm.

4) Y̆ bà-fɛd ba – These are my brothers/sisters.

Underline the verbs in the sentences below:

1) Sigala bɛn mɨ kù i – Sigala has broken his leg.
2) Bùma kêd nchì ndû mon – Buma has poured water on the baby.
3) Nǎ bɛti ŋgâ mon jɨ mɨ ɛ – Mother asked if the baby has eaten.

Exercise 3C: Grammar and Vocabulary with [ə] Sound
Underline the nouns in the sentences below:

1) Chi ma làŋ – Sit on the chair
2) Fa mɨ làŋ lɛ – Give me that chair
3) Gìma kôm tu mon nì kàm – Gima shaved the baby's hair with a razor blade.
4) Ba jûn bà-njàmbi ited ma ntan– Father has bought three sheep from the market.
5) Bà-ləm jam ma ŋgwɛn tì – There are lots of bats in the farm.

Underline the verbs in the sentences below:

1) Nǎ nì nləm ŋgɨ̀ŋ – Mother is grinding corn (fufu)
2) Kènnǎ kà chêd tɨ ma ŋgwɛn – Kenna felled a tree in the farm.
3) Kə nchì no – Get some water and drink.
4) Bà-njàmbi chàlî mànjì– The sheep have crossed the road.
5) Babila kàlî sòŋkù ì – Babila has hung his pants/trouser.

Exercise 3D: Spelling and Tones
Circle the misspelled words or those whose tones have not been properly marked. Then write the correct word on the line provided.

1) Ŋgwɛd kɛd mɨ ma laŋ ndab – Oil has spilled on the floor.

....

....

2) À bŏŋ mà chu chû mbikèd – It is good to speak the truth.

....

....

3) Kə chə'tu a nsǎm – Take my hat and hold.

....

....

4) Bàsogĕ nì mmâ' bɛd – The soldiers are at war.

....

5) Lesiga nì bà-fed itɛd. – Lesiga has three siblings

....

6) Dùna wâd bò i nì kəm – Duna has cut his hand with a razor blade.

....

Chapter Glossary

	Nouns	Verbs
[ɛ]	Bɛn – a dance Ŋgèn – grasshopper Ŋgwɛd – oil Ŋgwɛn – farm Mbikɛd – truth Bèd – war, struggle Mfɛd (singular) – brother/sister = bà-fɛd or fɛdfɛd (plural) brothers/sisters	Bɛn – to break Kĕd – to pour/ to spill Bɛti – to ask / to question, to beg Ləm – grind, pound; suffer injury Kɛn – to sigh

	Nouns	Verbs
[ə]	Ləm– bat Kə̀m – Razor, razor blade Lə̀ŋ – Chair Lə̀mì–lə̀mɨ – hide and seek Njə̀mbi – Sheep (singular), = bà-njə̀mbi – plural)	Lə̆m – to hide, something, conceal, bury Ləŋni (verb) – to swing, rinse Kə – to get, take, receive, take over, defend Kə̀li – to hang Chə̆d – to cut down, to fell (a tree) Lə̀mɨ – to hide oneself

NOTES

CHAPTER 4

I & Ɨ

In this chapter, we shall examine the vowels [i] and [ɨ] in Mungaka. The letter [i] is sounded in similar fashion as the vowel in the English word, beat /biyt/. The letter [ɨ] is isn't found in the English language but may be found in many other languages such as Turkish and Russian. Most languages in the western Grasslands of Cameroon have the [ɨ] sound as well. Let us take a closer look at these vowels below.

Lesson 4A: Practice the sounds of Speech

Read out the words in the first column, then read the words in the second column; then read the words in pairs contrasting the vowel sounds.

[i]	[ɨ]
Ji	Jɨ
Kiti	Kɨ
Li'	Lɨ̆'
Lĭn	Lɨ̆m
Bi, bĭ	Bɨ'
Fi	Fɨ
Mvi	Mvɨ

Lesson 4B: Grammar and Vocabulary with [i] Sound

[i] by itself may stand for a possessive pronoun in Mungaka.
ì – (possessive pronoun) – his, her;
i mfɛd ì – He is his brother/ She is her sister/ He or she is her sibling

i – (pronoun) – he, she, it;
i kà jûn nji – She bought a dress

I – (pronoun), him, her, it;
a tàb i – It is her shoe
Ì – (pronoun), who, which, whose;

Yɔ̀ tab bə ì wə ɛ? Whose shoe is this?
A ì Kè'bìla – It is Kehbila's
Yɔ̀ tab bə ì Kè'bìla – This shoe is Kehbila's

Underline the nouns in the sentences below:

4) Lilì num mɨ mômbɔd – A mosquito has bitten the baby.
5) Sèma ghâ mì' ma nì nsɛn – Sema says I have dark eyes.
6) Njə̀mbî yàb vî bon ited – Their sheep gave birth to three lambs.

Underline the verbs in the sentences below:

1) Bɔbga lǐn mà naŋ mbaŋ sě – Bobga can also cook
2) Mon kà li ma laŋndab – The baby slept on the floor
3) Bon fì'tî bâ yàb – The children are imitating their father.

Exercise 4C: Grammar and Vocabulary with [ɨ] Sound

Underline the nouns in the sentences below:

1) Ba ŋkɔm nì bà-mvɨ ited – Ba Nkom has three dogs.
2) Lɨ̀ŋ tî kə ɛ? – What is her/his name?
3) Lɨ̀ŋ ti a bə̂ Kèna – My name is Kenna
4) Lɨm mon bàŋbàŋ – The baby's tongue is red

Underline the verbs in the sentences below:

1) Bì to bà kɨb mbìyaŋ – Come let's crack some peanuts.
2) Fǐn nchùndab lɛ – Close (lock) that door.
3) Mon lɛ kɨ̂ tu tìtì – The child is too heady.
4) Ù kà tɨ̂ ŋkab i sə' ɛ? – How much did you pay?
5) Tɨ jòm lɛ kɨ jam yɔ̀ lùm bə – The plum tree hasn't borne any fruits this year.

Exercise 4D: Spelling and Tones

Circle the misspelled words or those whose tones have not been properly marked. Then write the correct word on the line provided.

1) Bɨsɨŋ jam mà fà' – There are a lot of birds in the farm.
    ....
    ....

2) Liŋ mvɨ à bə Max – My dog's name is Max
    ....
    ....

3) Bà-lɨ jam ma nchi tɨ – There are lots of tadpoles in the water.
    ....
    ....

Chapter Glossary

	Nouns	Verbs
[i]	Lilì – fly, mosquito Mi' – eyes (plural), (li') – eye (singular) Njèmbi – sheep Mbi (n) – goat Nchì – water Mvi – the world, universe Nji – dress, cloth Mândìkàŋ – umbrela	Lĭn – to know Fì'ti – to imitate, to copy Li – to sleep Vi – to give birth Kiti – to look, watch Bĭ – to plant, sow

	Nouns/Adjective	Verbs
[ɨ]	Mvɨ – Dog Lɨŋ – name Mɨsɨŋ – bird (singular, Bɨsɨŋ plural) Ghɨgha – butterfly Ghɨghàŋ – okra Lɨ – tadpole Tɨ – tree Ghɨghìn – clown, fool, jester Lɨm – sweet (**adjective**)	Fɨ̌n – to lock, close Ghɨ̌ – to laugh Jɨ – to eat Kɨ – to glow, burn Tɨ – to pay Kɨb – to crack (especially grains or nuts)

NOTES

CHAPTER 5

O, Ɔ & U

In this chapter, we shall examine the vowels [o], [ɔ] and [u] in Mungaka. The letter [o] is sounded as the vowel in the English word, coat /**kowt**/, [ɔ] as the vowel in the English word, caught /**kɔt**/ and [u] as the vowel in the English word, cooed /**kuwd**/. In this chapter, we shall learn how to distinguish the various vowels in spoken and written forms.

[**u**] by itself may stand for a second–person possessive or object/subject pronoun in Mungaka.

Ù – you, thou (subject)

Ù nâŋ mbaŋ ɛ? – Have you cooked something?

Ù – your, thy (possessive pronoun)

Yǒ ŋwà'nì ù – This is your book.

U – you, thee; (object pronoun)

Bo fuŋ u – you've been called.

Lesson 5A: Practice the sounds of Speech

Read out the words in the first column, then read the words in the second and third columns; then read the words in sequence contrasting the vowel sounds.

Bo	Bɔ'	Bu'
Bò	Bɔ̀'	fu'
Bom	Bɔm	bub
Fom	Fɔm	Fŭb
Ko	Kɔ'	Ku
Wom	Wɔm	Wu'
Lo	Lɔ̌'	Lun
To	Tɔŋ	Tuŋ
No	Nɔ̌'	Nu
Fò	Fɔ'	Fù

Exercise 5B: Grammar and Vocabulary with [o] Sound
Underline the nouns in the sentences below:

1) Ba nì mfâ' ma njàm ndab nì so – Father is working with a hoe in the backyard.
2) Bà sogè jam ma yɔ̀ ŋgɔ̀ŋ– There are so many soldiers in this country.
3) Nubia sě mɨ sòŋkù ì – Nubia has torn his pants.
4) Bon nì njɨ nì mbò mab – The kids are eating with their hands.

Underline the verbs in the sentences below:

1) Ba kôm tu Bùma à bɔ̀ŋ – Father gave Buma a nice haircut.
2) Dɔbgima nì ndu'ti mà bom ndab – Dobgima is learning how to build a house.
3) À bǒŋ mà no nchì ŋgɔ̀ŋ ndìb mɛ' – It is good to drink water all the time.
4) Bì to bà ghə ma ŋgwɛn – Come, let's go to the garden/farm.

Exercise 5C: Grammar and Vocabulary with [ɔ] Sound
Underline the nouns in the sentences below:

1) Sama kà ghê vum ma kɔ̀b – Sama went on a hunt in the forest.
2) Bà ti' fɔmmvi – See you tomorrow (Literally, it means we'll meet each other tomorrow).
3) Ba nì nto fɔmmvi – Father will come tomorrow.
4) Bì chi nì bɔnì – Stay well (Stay in peace).

Underline the verbs in the sentences below:

1) Ù lǒ' ya ɛ? – Where do you come/coming from?
2) Lǒ' ŋkɔŋ–ŋwà'nì lɛ mfa mɨ – Take that pen and give me.
3) Sadmia kǒŋ mà kɔ' tɨ – Sadmia loves to climb trees.
4) Ù bǒŋ a tì – I like you a lot (Literally, you please me a lot).

Exercise 5D: Grammar and Vocabulary with [u] Sound
Underline the nouns and/or pronouns in the sentences below:

1) Ù nâŋ mbaŋ ɛ? – Have you cooked something?
2) Yǒ ŋwà'nì ù – This is your book.
3) Nâ bò tɔ' mɨ tuŋ mon – Our mother has pierced the baby's ears.
4) Vu châmbo yɔ̀ ndìb – People die a lot these days. (So many deaths these days).
5) Kenna, u lùm i sə' ɛ? – Kenna, how old are you?

6) Yɔ̀ tundab nì nchwe tìtì – This roof is leaking a lot.
Underline the verbs in the sentences below:

1) Bòn/bon tum mɨ ma ndab mɛ' – Everyone/children have all gone out.
2) Mvɨ̂ ba kà nûm kù a – Father's dog bit my leg.
3) Ba kà jûn tab mfi mfi mbè̀ bon – Father bought new shoes for the children.

Exercises 5E: Spelling and Tones
Circle the misspelled words or those whose tones have not been properly marked. Then write the correct word on the line provided

1) Kùna ghâ i kɔŋ Kè'bùma – Kuna says she likes Kehbuma.

    ....

    ....

2) Nyǔm nì nta, lâ mfə' ni ŋkò – It's sunny and cold at the same time.

    ....

    ....

3) Bola kɔ̌ŋ mà naŋ mbàŋ – Bola likes to cook.

    ....

    ....

4) Tuŋ ti a nì njaŋ – My ear hurts.

    ....

    ....

5) Mɨ̀ nì mbɔ' bà-mvɨ – I'm scared of dogs.

    ....

    ....

Chapter Glossary

	Nouns	Verbs
[o]	So – a hoe Sogè – soldier Sòŋkù – pants/trouser Bo – hand Bon – children Mon – child Nyo – snake Fò – fon, chief Fom – to be rich, full	Kom– to cut, to carve, to shave Bom – to build, mold No – to drink To – to come Wom – to garden, make garden beds Lo – to rain Ko – to be affected by, feel, overcome with
	Nouns	**Verbs**
[ɔ]	Kɔb – forest, wood Fɔm– poverty Mbɔ' – peanut pudding Fɔmmvi – next day, tomorrow Bɔnì – peace, blessing, security Bɔm – belly, stomach Bɔ̀ŋ – goodness, kindness, beauty, good deeds Bɔ̀'tì – valley, plain Wɔ̀btì – ring Wɔm – 10 (ten) Bɔ̀'– mushroom	Lɔ̆' – to take, come from, derive from Kɔbti – to cover, close Kɔ̆ŋ – to love, like Fɔ̆m – to roast, also fɔmni (in hot ash or fire) Kɔ' – to climb, ascend Bɔ̆ŋ – to be good, to please Tɔŋ – to yell, shout Nɔ̆' – to lay down

	Nouns	**Verbs**
[u]	Tuŋ – ear	Tum – to go out
	Fù – medicine	Fuŋ – to call
	Vu – death	Fŭb – to sip
	Kun – bed	Num – to bite
	Lùm – year	Jun – to buy
	Tundab – roof	Kud – to tie
	Kuŋ – box	Ku – to die
	Lum – right side (foot/hand)	Nu – to drink (variant of no)
	Nyùm – Sun	Bu' – beat, bark, beg
	Vum – hunting	
	Bu' – bundle, packet	

NOTES

THE GLOTTAL STOP

The glottal stop is a speech sound that has lost its separate distinctiveness and occurs post–vocalic in speech as a feature of some vowels. It cannot be classified as a consonant or a vowel. In this chapter, we shall examine several categories of vowels and the glottal stops that accompany them. These include front close, front open, back close, back open, and central vowels.

Note that the glottal stop, when it occurs, often does so only after a vowel.

Front Close Vowel [i]

These are vowels produced at the front of the mouth with the tongue high/close.
- When a glottal stop follows this vowel in Mungaka, it often creates a tight, abrupt closure because the mouth is already in a narrow position.
- The result is a sharp break after the vowel.

Effect: *The vowel stays high and tense, and the glottal stop sounds crisp and clean.*

Front Close Vowels	Glottal Stop
Mǐ (to swallow)	Mi' (eyes)
Bì (kola nut)	Bi'ti (to repeat)
Mbin (cockroach)	Bì'ni (to start)
Fifi (a kind of vegetable/mushroom), (bɔ̌' fifi)	Fì'ti (to imitate)

---

1 This chapter has been completed thanks to notes compiled by Ba Ŋkɔm Gwannua Ndàŋgàm.

Front Open Vowel [a]

These vowels are made at the front but with the mouth wide open.
- Think of the vowel in "father" (/a/).
- When a glottal stop follows, the openness of the vowel makes the glottal stop feel heavier and more noticeable, because the vocal tract moves from wide open to a sudden closure.

Effect: *The vowel is long and open, then suddenly cut off.*

Kǎ (grandmother)	Kǎ' (to peel)
Ba (father)	Ba' (to weave)
Ma (elder sister)	Mǎ' (to rear animals, also to throw)
Tà (insect, fly)	Tǎ' (to search for something)
Wà (kind of tree)	Wa' (to throw away, discard)
Nǎ (mother)	Na'ti (to show)

Back Close Vowel [u]

These vowels are produced at the back of the mouth with the tongue high/close.
- Think of the vowel in "food" (/u/).
- When a glottal stop follows, the transition is from a rounded, back position to a throat closure, which can make the glottal stop sound slightly softer than after front vowels.

Effect: *A rounded, back vowel followed by a gentle but clear stop.*

Tu (head)	Tu' (to fetch water)
Bùmti (to meet)	Bu'ti (to rule, govern)
Jun (to buy)	Ju' (yams)
Lùm (year)	Lu' (wooden spoon)
Mǔd	Mu'

Front Close Vowel [e]

These are vowels produced at the front of the mouth with the tongue in a mid (not high) position.

- Think of the vowel in English "say," which is close to /e/.
- When a glottal stop follows this vowel in Mungaka, it creates a clear but not overly sharp closure because the mouth is moderately open.

Effect: *The result is a clean, medium-strength break after the vowel.*

Chènti (to urinate)	Chè'ni (to escort)
Kèmti (to economize)	Kè'ti (to untie)
Pèti (to find out)	Pè'ti (to wink)
Bèti (to sharpen)	Be'ti (to retail)
Jèn (lid)	Jè'ni (to breathe)

Back Open Vowel [ɔ]

These are vowels produced at the back of the mouth with the tongue in a low/open position.

- Think of the vowel in English "thought" or "law" (in accents that use /ɔ/).
- When a glottal stop follows this vowel in Mungaka, the wide, open mouth position makes the closure feel heavy and strongly marked, because the vocal tract moves from a large open space to a sudden stop.

Effect: *The result is a deep, weighty break after the vowel.*

Bɔ̀ŋ (beauty)	Mbɔ' (groundnut/peanut pudding)
Bɔnì (blessings)	Bɔ̀'tì (valley)
Kɔ̀ŋ (spear)	Kɔ̀' (bridge)
Mbɔ̂ŋtu (brain)	Mɔ̀' (another one)
Pɔb (initiate)	Bɔ̀' (mushroom)

Central Close Vowel [ɨ]

These vowels /ɨ/ and /ə/ are produced in the middle of the mouth, neither front nor back.

- Think of the vowel in "sofa" (/ə/) or a neutral central vowel.
- When a glottal stop follows, the transition is very natural because the tongue is already in a neutral, relaxed position.

Effect: *The glottal stop feels smooth and natural, often marking boundaries between morphemes or syllables.*

Mbɨkɛd (bad, evil)	Mbɨ' (raw)
Tìn (strength, power)	Tɨ'ti (to advise)
Bɨn (breast)	Bɨ' (us, pronoun)
Jɨ (to eat)	Njɨ' (egusi)

Central Vowel [ə]

Fə̀ti (rest)	Fə'ti (tasty)
Jə̌ (to steal)	Jə̀tì (broom)
Kə̀m (razor)	Lə'tì (introductory dance by men about to fire guns)
Kə (to take, receive)	Kə̀'ti (to limp)

NOTES

NOTES

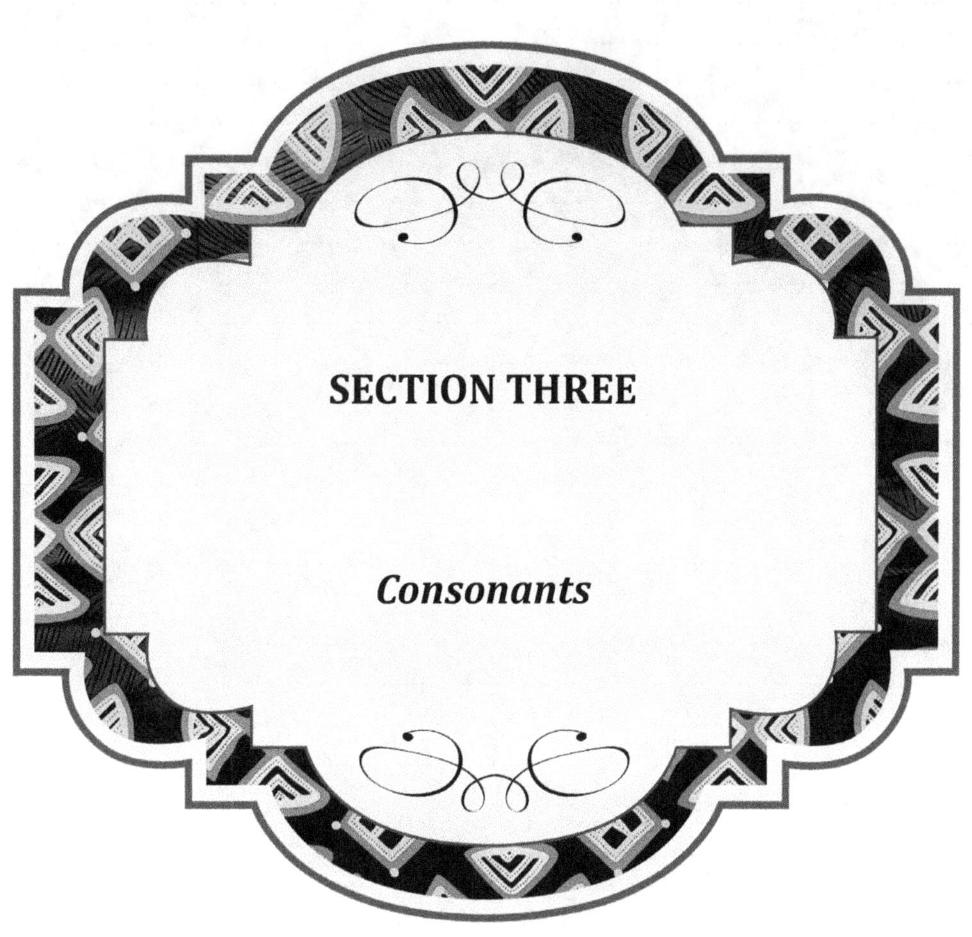

SECTION THREE

Consonants

NOTES

CHAPTER 7

P & B

In this chapter, we shall examine the consonants [p] and [b] in Mungaka. The letter [p] is sounded in similar fashion as the consonant in the English word, pig /**pig**/ and [b] is sounded as the consonant in the English word, big /**big**/. Both [p] and [b] are known as **bilabial consonants** which means that in sounding them, the speaker uses both lips to create the sound. As a matter of convention, Mungaka words that end with a bilabial consonant always end with a [b] rather than a [p] – e.g. tab, ndab, ŋkab, kɔb etc.

Lesson 7A: Practice the sounds of Speech

Read out the words in the first column, then read the words in the second column; then read the words in pairs contrasting the vowel sounds.

[p]	[b]
Pab	Bab
Păd	Bĕd
Pa'	Ba'
Pèti	Bèti
Pĭ	Bĭ
Pub	Bub
Păŋ	Băŋ
Pib	Bim

Exercise 7B: Grammar and Vocabulary with [p] Sound

Underline the nouns in the sentences below:

1) Bon kà wê pepè nìŋkù' – The children caught a swallow yesterday.
2) Mɔ̆' pəm nì nji à – There's a blot on my dress

Underline the verbs in the sentences below:

1) Fìfə̂d pâd ndab – The storm knocked down the house.
2) To mpad u nì ŋkwèn à– Come let me put you on my back.
3) Babila kà pèti nù lɛ – Babila investigated the matter.
4) I pèti ndìb bə kà vi mon lɛ a – S/he questioned the child's date of birth.
5) Ma mpǐ' yɔ̀ kaŋ bə – Don't make a dent on this bowl.

Exercise 7C: Grammar and Vocabulary with [b] Sound

Underline the nouns in the sentences below:

1) Mbǎb majǐ bàm – A mouse is in the bag.
2) Tab mon majǐ ndab – The baby's shoes are in the house.
3) Yɔ̀ bə kwà' ŋguli bàtì – This is a great idea.

Underline the verbs in the sentences below:

1) Nà'vòma batî nǎ i ma ntan – Nahvoma followed her mother to the market.
2) Dinga batî nsun ì ma ŋgwɛn– Dinga followed his friend to the farm.
3) Bon ŋgɔb bati mɨ nâ yàb – The chicks have followed the hen.
4) Bà bàtî nù lɛ mbɔ̀ŋkɛd – We've thought about this matter very well.
5) Bèti kɨkà' mfa mɨ̀ – Sharpen the stick and give it to me
6) Bèti pencil lɛ mfa mɨ̀ – Sharpen the pencil and give it to me

Exercise 7D: Spelling and Tones

Circle the misspelled words or those whose tones have not been properly marked. Then write the correct word on the line provided.

1) Sama bamti nyǔŋtù i – Sama had a haircut.

   ....

   ....

2) Ni Dɔb bâmti mɨ tu Babila – Ni Dob has given Babila a haircut.

   ....

   ....

3) Bobga bùbti mɨ tab i – Bobga has spoiled his shoes.

   ....

4) I pǐ' mɨ mbàŋ lɛ – S/he has made a dent on the pot.

....

....

5) Ma mpaŋ jubàŋ lɛ bə – don't cut off the potato.

....

....

Chapter Glossary

	Nouns/Adjective	Verbs
[p]	Pepè – swallow Pàdŋkwèn – knapsack, backpack, rug sack Pəm – spot, blur, blot Pəmtu – bald head, bald–headed Pepà – paper (derived from English) Pub – (**adj**) – white (as snow)	Păd – put a load on one's back or shoulder; also to overthrow, knock down something. Pèti – question, investigate Pǐ' – press in, break in, make a dent; Pàti – beat off, dust off Păŋ – to cut off a piece, chip something with a knife Pě – to find out, question, examine Papìla – to deliberate, reflect, consider, ponder Pa' – to become spoiled (of food) Pìti (also pì'ti) – cut into small pieces

	Nouns	Verbs
[b]	Bàm – bag Mbàb– mouse Bìchaŋ – a kind of vegetable Bàtì – a thought or idea/suggestion Bo – hand, arm Bɔbŋgìŋ – flour (of wheat or maize) – also bɔŋgìŋ Ndab– house Mbaŋ – pot Jubàŋ – potato	Bàti– to think, to suggest Bèti – to sharpen Bamti – to cut (hair) Bati– to follow Bubti – to spoil, destroy Bǐ – to plant, sow Běd – to refuse, deny Băŋ – be red, yellow, fly into passion Bim – to accept, agree Ba' – to weave, plait Bab – to warm, roast, dry

NOTES

CHAPTER 8

T & D

In this chapter, we shall examine the consonants [t] and [d] in Mungaka. The letter [t] is sounded in similar fashion as the consonant in the English word, top /**top**/ and the letter [d] in similar fashion as the consonant in the English word, dog /**dog**/. Note that no Mungaka words end with the letter [t]. If you are tempted to spell a word that sounds like it ends with a [t], then use [d]. Examples include mbɔ̀ŋkɛd, kĕd, tud, ŋgwɛd etc. We shall examine these sounds closely below.

Lesson 8A: Practice the Sounds of Speech
Read out the words in the first column, then read the words in the second column; then read the words in pairs contrasting the vowel sounds.

[t]	[d]
Tŏn	Dŏ
Tu	Du
Tăŋ	Dăŋ
Tĕ	Dĕ
Tɨ̌'	Dɨ̌'

Exercise 8B: Grammar and Vocabulary with [t] Sound
Underline the nouns in the sentences below:
1) Nă jûn tâb mfi mbè Babila – Mother bought a pair of new shoes for Babila.
2) Dɔb nì ŋkiti TV ma tali – Dob is watching TV in the living room.
3) Tita lɛ ta tìtì – The pepper is very hot.
4) Ŋgòndam lɛ nì chàŋtì njamɨ – The bride is very pleased.

Underline the verbs in the sentences below:

1) Bola nì ntaŋti nì chû bà'nì – Bola counts in the Bali language (Mungaka).
2) Bon nì ntasɨ' kɨmvi – The children are playing outside.
3) I tànî nù – S/he doubts the matter.
4) Nǎ nì nteti ŋkun mɨkali – Mom is selecting rice grains.

Exercise 8C: Grammar and Vocabulary with [d] Sound
Underline the nouns in the sentences below:

1) Bì du'ti ŋwà'nì mbɔ̀ŋkɛd – Study/learn well.
2) Yɔ̀ dù'tì lɛ bɔtɨ kwà' tìtì – This study/research is very simple.
3) Bì ye bà du'ti chû Bà'nì – Let us learn the Mungaka language.

Underline the verbs in the sentences below:

1) Mon du mɨ ma laŋ ndab – The baby has thrown up on the floor.
2) Ù bɛ̌ njɨ njamɨ, ù du – If you eat a lot, you will throw up.
3) Dù ta mɨ Bùma – Buma has been stung by a bee.

Exercise 8D: Spelling and Tones
Circle the misspelled words or those whose tones have not been properly marked. Then write the correct word on the line provided.

1) Bòn ba lad mɨ du lɛ mɛ' – My children have eaten all the honey.

2) Dù' Bobga nì njaŋ – Bobga's waist hurts.

3) Yǎ na nì ndu'ti Kenna mà naŋ baŋ – My mother is teaching Kenna how to cook.

4) Mɨn lɛ wu' tì – This man is very big.

Chapter Glossary

	Nouns/Adverb	Verbs
[t]	Tita – pepper	Tăd – to jump, hop, leap
	Tìtì – very, much (form of tì)	Tŏn – to be or become hot, fierce
	Tăŋndab – ceiling (also, kɨtàŋ)	Tasɨ' – to play, gamble, game
	Tab – shoe, boot, sandal	Tàni – to doubt, oppose, contradict, criticize
	Tàmnsòn– frog	Taŋti – to count
	Tìd – small worms, maggots, mites	Tă – to fly, squirt
	Tali – dining room for men, living room	Tenikɛd – run off
	Tìtɔ' – toad	Teti – to elect, select
	Tàd – big pot	Ten – run off, escape, run away
	Tìtà – an honorary name for grown up princes and appointed officials of non–royal descent).	Tɨ̆' – to become silent, speechless
	Tuŋ – ear	Tĕ – to smooth, polish, glide, slide, lick inside of pot with finger
	Tu – head	Tăŋ – to be tough, tenacious, clinch
	Tɨ – tree	
	Tì – very, much (**adv**)	

	Nouns	Verbs
[d]	Dù (noun)– honey/ honeybee	Dŏg – to fight
	Dɔg – a fight	Dù'ti – to study
	Dù'tì – a lesson, a study	Du – to throw up, vomit
	Du' (noun) – waist	Dăŋ – to claim everything for one's self
	Du – vomit)	Dĕ – to slander, backbite
	Dŏ – grandfather	Dɨ̆' – to wind, twist

NOTES

CHAPTER 9

K, G & GH

In this chapter, we shall look at two letters and one sound combination (K, G & GH). The letter [k] is sounded in a same fashion as the consonant in the English word, cot /**cot**/. This letter is the first of five velar consonants or sound combinations we shall examine in this workbook. A velar consonant is a consonant that is pronounced with the back part of the tongue against the soft palate. The other velar consonants in Mungaka include ŋ, g, gh and w.

Similarly, letter [**g**] is sounded in the same fashion as the consonant in the English word got /**got**/.

We shall also examine the sound combination [**gh**] which our basic learners may face some difficulty with because the sound combination is not found in the English alphabet. It is the third of the velar consonants or sound combinations we shall examine in this workbook. It was previously represented in the old German alphabet as [ɤ]. We shall examine each of these letters and sound combination separately in this chapter. But first, let us do some sound practice.

Lesson 9A: Practice the sounds of Speech

Read out the words in the first column, then read the words in the first, second and third columns; then read the words in pairs contrasting the consonant sounds.

[K]	[G]	[GH]
Kun	Gag	Ghâ'
Kab	Gàŋ	Ghə
Kiti	Ŋgɨm	Ghǎ
Kè	Ŋgàŋndab	Ghɨ
Kǔ'	Ŋgɔb	Ghǎŋ
Kad	Ŋgàb	Ghan
Kùbtì	Ŋgàm	Ghɨ̀n

[K]	[G]	[GH]
Kɔ̀b	Ŋgab	Ghàŋ
Kàti	Geb	Ghàb

Exercise 9B: Grammar and Vocabulary with [K] Sound

Underline the nouns in the sentences below.

1) Njì ba majǐ kuŋ – My clothes are in the box.
2) Kǎ to nì kûŋ mfi mbɛ̀ Lima – Grandmother has brought a new box for Lima.
3) Kějɨ lɛ mǐ mɨ – The food is finished.

Underline the verbs in the sentences below.

1) Kè'mia kà kêm sànjàb – Kehmia squeezed the huckleberry.
2) Dɔb kan mɨ – Dob is tired.
3) Kùna kab mɨ tita lɛ – Kuna has harvested the pepper.
4) Lɜ̀ma kan (mɨ) mà tǎd – Lema is exhausted from jumping.

Exercise 9C: Grammar and Vocabulary with [G] Sound

Underline the nouns in the sentences below.

1) Bà gwè jam kɨntèd tì – There are so many jesters in the palace.
2) Gàŋ bɵ̂ yum mà jɔ̌b nchì – The flute is an instrument for singing/ The flute is a musical instrument
3) Gwǎnyìnyi kà kwêd mbì ba mɛ' – A hyena killed all my goats/ A hyena ate all my goats.
4) Gàna bɵ̂ mû gwè – Gana is a jester's son.

Underline the verbs in the sentences below.

5) Ba kà gɵ̂b nyàm lɛ kwà' mbɔ̀ŋkɛd – Father aimed at the animal very well.
6) Bùma kà jǐd ŋkan mbì'ni mà gəbli – Buma got tired from walking and began to stagger.

Exercise 9E: Grammar and Vocabulary with [gh] Sound

Underline all the nouns and adverbs in the sentences below.

1) Bàghan jɵ̂ ŋkàb a mɛ' – Thieves stole all my money.
2) Lena châm nchì majǐ ghə – Lena is carrying water in a calabash.
3) Lǎ ghâ' – Pass here!

4) To ghâ' – Come here

5) Mɨ nì nchi ma ghâ' – I live here

Exercise 9F: Spelling and Tones

Circle the misspelled words or those whose tones have not been properly marked. Then write the correct word on the line provided

1) Ba gâ ù to – Dad says you should come.

....

....

2) Ù gha kə? – What did you say?

....

....

3) Babila ghà i lùm itan – Babila says he is five years old.

....

....

4) Dɔb gha i kan mɨ – Dob says he's tired.

....

....

5) Bo kà ghè ma Bamenda – They went to Bamenda.

....

....

6) Bùma ghə ma ndâ-ŋwà'nì – Buma has gone to school.

....

....

7) Ba kàb sànjàb – Let's harvest some huckleberry.

....

....

Chapter Glossary

	Noun	**Verb**
[K]	Kuŋ – box, coffin	Kan – to be tired, become tired, exhausted or fatigued
	Kǎ – grandmother	Kaŋ – roast, bake, fry
	Kějɨ – food (plural), meal	Kàti – to draw, sketch
	Kě – things, items,	Kom – smoothen, plane, carve, hew, shave
	Kè – mat	Kàti – to draw
	Kam – crab	Kem – squeeze, press, milk

	Noun	Verb
[K]	Kun – bed Kuŋ – box, trunk, coffin Kwàtad – seven Kə̀m – razor Kù – foot kùm –masquerade Kŭ' – cocoayam Kùbtì – wooden bowl Kɔ̀b – belt	Kab– to harvest (vegetable) Kiti – to look Kad – to visit, also mà kani
	Noun	**Verb**
[G]	Gwè – jester, clown Gàŋ – Flute, mouth organ Gwǎnyìnyi – hyena Ŋgɨm – locust Ŋgàŋndab – house owner Ŋgàb – week Ŋgɔb – chicken Ŋgab – antelope	Gəb – to aim at (with a gun or spear) Gəbli – to stagger, (especially due to sick feet) Gag – to be disobedient
	Nouns/Adverb	**Verb**
[Gh]	Ghâ' – here (**adv**) Ghan – thief (pl. Bà-ghan) ghə – ladle, calabash Ghə̀' – envy, greed Ghìghìn – clown, fool, jester Ghə̀ghə' – center Gha' – bark, bowl; outermost Gha'tɨ – bark of a tree Ghàŋ – chest Ghìghàŋ – okra Ghì – laughter	Gha – to say, to affirm (also see suŋ) Ghɛ̌ – to go, to depart Ghǎŋ – wind with something, bind Ghàŋni – to swell (of the body) Ghàbti – to share, divide Ghèmti – to help Ghǎm – to spread, cover densely Ghɨ̌ – to laugh

Noun	Verb
Ghàlà' – scaffold, framework, brickwork, debris of something, skeleton Ghìn plural of ŋgìn –visitor Ghàb – share, portion	

NOTES

CHAPTER 10

CH & J

In this chapter we shall focus on two letters/sound combination: [**ch**] and [**j**]. Note that the Mungaka language does not have a stand–alone letter [c] or [h]. The sound combination [ch] has the same sound or pronunciation as in the English word /**chuck**/ and letter [c] is always followed by the letter [**h**]. On the other hand, letter J has the same pronunciation as in the English word /**jug**/. In the old Mungaka alphabet, the [j] sound was represented as [dz]. This has been simplified in the New Alphabet as [j].

Lesson 10A: Practice the sounds of Speech

Read out the words in the first column, then read the words in the second column; then read the words in pairs contrasting the consonant sounds.

[CH]	[J]
Cho	Jab
Chǎ	Jǎ
Chu	Jun
Chu'	Jaŋ
Chǎd	Jŏb
Chi	Juŋ
Chě	Ji
Chɔ'	Jɔb
Cham	Jam
Chi'	Ji'

Exercise 10B: Grammar and Vocabulary with [ch]

Underline the nouns in the sentences below.

1) Chi lɛ nyĭm mɨ – The salt has melted
2) Nɨŋ chi ma mbaŋ – Put some salt in the pot.
3) Kɔ̆d chèn ti u – Touch your forehead
4) I kûd chèn ti i – He/she is frowning.
5) Chaŋ nì kǔ mvɨ – There is a chain on the dog's foot.

Underline the verbs in the sentences below.
1. Bisona châb ŋkun-màli majĭ mbaŋ – Bisona soaked beans in the pot.
2. Bo châb nji ma nchì, nji bì'ni mà sǔ' – They soaked their clothes in water before washing them.
3. A mà mbɔ̆ŋ mà chăb mɨn bə – It is not good to insult someone.
4. Mon chènti ma laŋndab – The baby urinated on the floor
5. Ŋkûndù' kà chènti nì sòŋkù ì – A drunk urinated in his pants.
6. Bo chè'ni mɨ ŋgònndam – They have escorted the bride.
7. To ŋgǎ nchè'ni a ma ŋgwɛn – Accompany me to the farm.

Exercise 10C: Grammar and Vocabulary with [j]

Underline the nouns in the sentences below.

1) Yɔ̀ jaŋ lɛ tĭn tìtì – This illness is so severe.
2) Jaŋ châmbo ma mvi – There are a lot of illnesses in the world.
3) ŋkwin jaŋjaŋ mà mbɔ̆ŋ bə – This wood is not a good one.
4) Jùŋ yab tŏn tì – Their hut is very hot.

Underline the verbs in the sentences below.

1) Babila nì njə̀' ndab nì jə̀'tì – Babila is sweeping the floor with a broom.
2) To njə̀'ti kù a – Come and clean my foot.
3) Nǎ jun mɨ tab mfi mbə̀ Bola – Mother has bought a new pair of shoes for Bola.
4) Kenna lĭn mà jɔ̆b nchì – Kenna can sing.

Exercise 10D: Spelling and Tones

Circle the misspelled words or those whose tones have not been properly marked. Then write the correct word on the line provided

1) Babila nì njè' ndab nì je'tì – Babila is sweeping the floor with a broom.

   ....

   ....

2) Yɔ̀ mon lɛ chǐt tì – This child is too hyperactive.

   ....

   ....

3) Bobga bubti mɨ jə'ti lɛ – Bobga has destroyed the broom.

   ....

   ....

4) Ma ŋkud chen ti u bə – Do not frown.

   ....

   ....

5) Ba chi ma chenmu' – Father is sitting by the fireside.

   ....

   ....

Chapter Glossary

	Noun	Verb
[CH]	Chen – forehead	Chǎb – to soak, steep, to insult
	Chaŋ – chain (jewelry)	Chènti – to urinate, to pee
	Chàŋtì – enjoyment, joy, pleasure	Cho – to enter
	Chaŋ – prison Ŋgàŋ–chaŋ– a prisoner	Chəli (v) to cross
	Chěnmu' – fireside	Chè'ni – to escort, send off, accompany
	Chinji – soap	Cham– to carry
		Chɨ̌' – to shake; also chɨ̌'ti
	Chu – talk	Chǎ – (of water) become very hot
	Chi – salt	Chu' – to pound
		Chǎd – to cut
		Chě – to arrive
		Chɔ' – to remove
		Chi' – to keep

	Noun	**Verb**
[J]	Jə̀'tì – broom	Jə̀'ti– to sweep
	Jaŋjaŋ – a species of tree	Jǒ – to steal, to overcome
	Juŋ – hurt	Jun – to buy, bargain
	Jaŋ– illness	Jɨ – to eat, inherit, enjoy
	Jɔ̀b – song	Jɔ̆b – to sing
	Jɔŋ – cone	Jǐd – to walk
		Jŭb – to peel
		Jaŋ – to be ill/sick
		Jɔ̀ŋni – to shout

CHAPTER 11

F & V

The letters F and V are known as Labiodental consonants – meaning that in order to sound them, we use our lower lips and upper teeth. These letters in Mungaka are sounded in a similar fashion as in English.

Lesson 11A: Practice the sounds of Speech
Read out the words in the first column, then read the words in the second column; then read the words in pairs contrasting the consonant sounds.

[F]	[V]
Fa	və
fə'	Və
fŭb	vŭ
fuŋ	Vaŋ
Fà'	Vu
Fù	Vù
Fĭn	Vin
Fə'ti	və'ti

Exercise 11B: Grammar and Vocabulary with [F]
Underline the adjectives in the sentences below.

1) Bo wê' njî fufu – They're wearing white clothes.
2) Ŋ-kɨ nchi ba nì fɔm – I am broke, I am lonely
3) I fɔm kwà' tìtì– He is very poor.
4) Nchì lɛ fə tì – The water is too cold.
5) Nă nâŋ nyàm, à fə'tì – The meat that mother cooked was very delicious.

Underline the nouns in the sentences below.

1) Yɔ̀ chu bə̂ kwà' fə̆bsuŋ – This is a big lie.
2) Ba ghə̆ mɨ ma lɨ̆' fà' – Father has gone to work.
3) Mon nì ŋwaŋni mà jɨ nì fɨkəb – The baby is trying to eat with spoon.
4) Fu'tu kɔbti mɨ lɨ̀' mɛ' – Places are all covered with fog.

Underline the verbs in the sentences below.

1) Fa kĕjɨ mbə̀ bon bo jɨ – Give some food to the kids to eat.
2) Bùma kà fûŋ ŋwà'nì, à lan – Buma read the book very well.
3) Ba nì mfûb ndù' ma tali – Father is sipping a drink in the living room.

Exercise 11C: Grammar and Vocabulary with [V]

Underline the nouns in the sentences below.

1) Yɔ̀ vàvà wu' tìtì – This waterfall is very big
2) Bà-ba kà ghə̂ vum nì ŋkù' – The fathers went hunting yesterday.
3) Nă nâŋ vub boà kàsiŋga – Mother cooked bitterleaf and cassava.
4) Ba boà Nă ghə̂ vu ma Njɛnkà' – Father and mother went to Njenka for a funeral.
5) Vŭtu bə̂ jâŋ mbɨkɛd – Epilepsy is a dangerous disease.

Underline the verbs in the sentences below

1) U bə̆ njɨ njɛd, u və̀' – You burp when you eat to your satisfaction.
2) Babila, mbu' mbo, və'ti mu' lɛ – Babila, please turn off the lights.
3) Kenna və'ti mɨ tâ' bă' tàb i – Kenna has lost one of her shoes.
4) Mvɨ̂ yàb vi mɨ bon ikwà – Their dog has given birth to four puppies.

Underline the adjectives in the sentences below.

1) Ndâ bòn ba vàgli tìtì– My children's room is too disorganized.
2) Bì ma ni njab ndab vàglivaglì bə! – Don't always leave your house in a disorderly/disorganized state.

Exercise 11D: Spelling and Tones

Circle the misspelled words or those whose tones have not been properly marked. Then write the correct word on the line provided

1) To bà fùŋ ŋwà'nì Nyìkɔ̀b – Come let us read the Bible.

....

....

2) Mì' mu fù' mὲ pab – Your face is very white.

....

....

3) Ba kà ghê vùm, ŋkwe mɔmɔm – Father went hunting and came back empty–handed.

....

....

4) Fǔ vǔtù bê kə ɛ? – What is the cure for epilepsy?

....

....

Chapter Glossary

		Noun/Adjective	Verb
[F]		Fà'–work, job	Fa – to give
		Fɨkəb – spoon	Fə'– to blow
		Fǎbsuŋ (also fàb) – lie (s)	Fǔb – to sip
		Fətì – rest	Fuŋ – to read
		Fu'tu – fog	Fǐn – to sell
		Fufu–white (adj.)	
		Fə'ti– to be tasty (adj.)	
		Noun/Adjective	**Verb**
[V]		Vin (grass for roofing)	Vi (v) – to give birth
		Vu– death	Və'ti – to put out (of fire)
		Vù – fall	Vǔ – to fall
		Vaŋnì – disorder	
		Vàvà also nchǐ vàvà – waterfall	
		Vum/vɨm – hunting	
		Vub/vɨb – a type of vegetable	

	Noun/Adjective	Verb
	Vŭtu – epilepsy, seizure Vaŋ – palm leave Vàgli/vàglivaglì (adj) disorganized, scattered	

S & M

In this section, we shall be examining two sets of consonants. Both letters [**m**] and [**s**] are pronounced the same as in English. The same principles that apply to other consonants in Mungaka remain the same for these letters.

Lesson 12A: Practice the sounds of Speech

Read out the words in the first column, followed by those in the second column; then read the words in pairs, contrasting the consonant sounds.

[M]	[S]	[Mf]*	[Mb]
Màd	Sàd	Mfɨŋ	Mbàb
Mǐ	Sǐ	Mfi	Mbùm
Mǎ'	Sǎ'	Mfòn	Mbin
Mè'ti	Sèbti	Mfɔ̀ŋ	Mbaŋ
Mǒm	Som	Mfə	Mban
Mǔd	Sǔd	Mfɨnyùm	Mbìchɔ̀'

** Some Mungaka learners may find it difficult saying words that start with [mf]. Read and practice the above while paying close attention to the [mf] and [mb] sounds.*

Let us examine a few important grammatical principles on the sound [m]:
Mà – infinitive marker – normally precedes a verb (mà jɨ, mà cham*)* etc.

Mâ – Maternity, mother
A second set of meaning for [**mâ**] could be an adjective, e.g. something big, great, important; e.g. mândâŋgɨ – a big house;

Exercise 12B: Grammar and Vocabulary with [m]
Underline the nouns in the sentences below.

1) Mălàm lɛ san mɨ – The mirror is broken.
2) Dǒ jûn mândìkàŋ mfi – Grandpa bought a new umbrella.
3) Ŋgwi à nɨ̂ŋ mbà' ni nji à – My wife attached a button to my dress (gown).
4) Mbà' tum mɨ nì nji Bola – A button came off Bola's dress.
5) Mànjì lɛ tèli tìtì – The road is very slippery.
6) Gima kà wê mɨsɨŋ nìŋkù'– Gima caught a bird yesterday.

Underline the Verbs in the sentences below.

1) Beb m-mâ' nji ǎ bà tum– A moment, let me dress up (put on) my clothes before we go out.
2) Mvɨ̂ Babila mî' kən nì bò a – Babila's dog snatched the bone from my hand.
3) Mon bĕd mà mĭ fù lɛ – The child refused to take the medicine.
4) Ma màŋni bi à bòn bə – Do not compare with people.

Underline the adjective in the sentences below.

1) Njî mon mĕn tìtì – The baby's cloth is dirty.

Exercise 12C: Grammar and Vocabulary with [mb/mf]
Underline the nouns in the sentences below.

1) Mfòn cho mɨ ma ntèd – The chief has entered the palace.
2) Mfə' nì ŋko a – I am feeling cold.
3) Ŋgɔb nyɨ̂ mbùm itàn – The chicken has laid 5 eggs.
4) Ŋu nì nta nì mfɨnyùm – The moon shines at night.
5) Mbàb bɘ̂ nyàm mbɨkɛd – A rat is a bad animal.

Exercise 12D: Grammar and Vocabulary with [s]
Underline the nouns in the sentences below.

1) Nă jun mɨ sàd mfi ma ntan – Mother has bought a new comb at the market store.
2) Săŋ nì nta mbɔ̀ŋkɛd nì mfɨnyùm – A star shines well at night.
3) Nă nâŋ ŋgɨŋ boà sànjàb – Mother has cooked fufu and vegetable

4) Kenna bê mɔ̌' tâ' nsun à – Kenna is one of my friends
5) Nchǐ sâ'nsi bɔ̌ŋ mà no – Spring water is good for drinking.

Exercise 12E: Grammar and Vocabulary with [s]
Underline the nouns in the sentences below.

1) Nǎ kà jûn so ì mfi – Mother bought a new hoe.
2) Saŋ mvɨ nì njaŋ i – The dog's tail is hurting.
3) Kud sòŋkǔ à tɨn – Tie your pants firmly.
4) Bà sogè ghê bèd – The soldiers have gone to war.

Underline the verbs in the sentences below.

1) Nǎ nì nsâd tu mon, nji ba' – Mother combs the baby's hair before braiding
2) À bɔ̌ŋ mà sǔ' bo ŋgɔ̀ŋ ndìb mɛ' – It is good to wash one's hands all the time.
3) Sema sě mɨ sòŋkù ì mfi lɛ – Sema has torn his new pants.

Exercise 12F: Spelling and Tones
Circle the misspelled words or those whose tones have not been properly marked. Then write the correct word on the line provided

1) Mɨ nì sìku wɔm – I have ten toes.

....

....

2) Mɨ̌n nì sìbo wɔm – Humans have ten fingers.

....

....

3) I bê kwà' ŋguli ŋgàn–tuŋ si – He is a good gravedigger.

....

....

4) Mbaŋ lɛ bǎŋ mɨ – The palm nut is ripe.

....

....

5) So bò u majɨ̌ bàm a – Put your hand into my pocket.

....

....

Chapter Glossary

	Noun/Adjective	Verb
[M]	Mbă' mbà' – morning	Mòmti – to touch, give opinion on
	Mɨsɨŋ – bird (plural–bɨsɨŋ)	Mǒ – to chat (round the fire), to have a good time, hang out
	Mànjì –road	Mă' – to throw, cast, put on
	Màd– manner	Màŋni – to compare
	Mbà' – button	Mè'ti – to finish
	Mândikaŋ – umbrella	Mǒm– to touch
	Mălàm –mirror	Mŭd – to be swollen
	Màŋnì – comparison	Mĭ' – to snatch, snap at
	Mfɨŋ – wound, scar	Mèni– to dirty, to soil
	Mfi – new, also puss	
	Mfòn – Chief, also fò	
	Mfɔ̀ŋ – dwarf cow	
	Mfə – fresh, cold	
	Mfɨnyùm – night	
	Mfə'– air, cold, fever, wind	
	Mbàb – mouse	
	Mbùm – body	
	Mbin – Cockroach	
	Mban – wound, sore	
	Mbaŋ – pot	
	Mbìchɔ̀' – baboon	
	Mĕn – dirty (adj.)	

	Noun/Adjective	Verb
[S]	Sâ'nsi – spring (water)	Sǎd – to comb
	Sikù – toe	Sǔ' – to wash, to clean
	Sibo – finger	Sě – to tear
	Sàd – comb	Sǐ – to pass gas
	Sàŋ – a star	Sǎ' to snatch
	Sì (tu sì) – tomb, grave	Sèbti – to reduce
	Sànjàb – huckleberry	Sǎd – to comb
	Saŋni– to be friendly (adj.)	Sènti –to resolve, to fix
	Nsun – a friend	Sànti –to scatter
		Som – to make a hissing sound intended to snub
		Sǔd– to peel

NOTES

CHAPTER 13

N, NY & ŋ

In this section of the book, we will focus on three sounds or sound combinations/letters common in written and spoken Mungaka – n, ny, ŋ. You will learn how to use and sound out the letters or sound combinations as well as the principles that govern the use of the curved [ŋ].

The letter [n] has a nasal sound. To produce it, place your tongue at the upper part of your mouth, just behind your top teeth and let the air through your nose, just as you would in English.

Lesson 13A: Practice the sounds of Speech

Read out the words in the first column, followed by those in the second column; then read the words in pairs, contrasting the consonant sounds. Do same for the last two columns.

[n]	NY	[ŋ]	
Na	Nyam	Ŋa'	Ŋu
Nă	Nyăb	Ŋɔ̆'	Ŋom
Nà'ti	Nya'ti	Ŋkab	Ŋkan
Ni	Nyăm	Ŋkɔ̀d	Ŋkə̀
Nɔ̆ŋ	Nyin	Ŋku	Ŋkɔ̀ŋ
Nɨŋ	nyo	Ŋkɨ	Ŋkù
Naŋ	Nyɔ'	Ŋka'	Ŋku'
Num	Nya'		
	Nyɨ̆'		

Principles that determine the use of [ŋ]

[ŋ] is one of the velar consonants, including [g] and [k]. These are consonants that are pronounced with the back part of the tongue touching the soft palate. An important principle is that [ŋ] is commonly used in words whose endings tend to sound like the [–ing] in English – e.g. **kuŋ**, **mbɨŋ**, **tuŋ**, **luŋ**, **lə̀ŋ** etc. [ŋ] is also a prenasal variant of mɨ – e.g. **ŋŋwà'ni** – I write; **ŋgə̌ mɨ** – I'm leaving;

NB: where the verb does not begin with a velar consonant, the regular [**n**] is used – as in: ncha'ti.

Exercise 13B: Grammar and Vocabulary with [ŋ]
Underline the nouns in the sentences below.

1) Ŋkan nì nten bòn (bùn) – The monkey runs away from people.
2) Ŋu nì nta – The moon is bright/The moon is out.
3) Ŋgàm lɛ lɨ̌m – This is an interesting conversation.
4) Ba ghə̂ vum, ntam ŋgàn – Father went hunting and killed a crocodile.

Underline the verbs in the sentences below.

1) Ŋa'a nchùndab lɛ – Open that door.
2) Ŋwà'ni lɨ̀ŋ ti u – Write your name.
3) Bola ŋə̂' mon – Bola has pinched the baby.
4) Ba ŋatî mbên vin iba– Father rolled the bundles of grass (for roofing).

Exercise 13C: Grammar and Vocabulary with [n]
Underline the nouns in the sentences below.

1) Njì kà jâŋ mon tìtì– The baby was very hungry.
2) Sama mèni mɨ nji ì – Sama has soiled his clothes.
3) Nǎ bìni mɨ lə̀' ma lɨ̌' fa' – Mother has returned from work.
4) Lɨŋ yǎ ni bə̂ Sigala – My big brother's name is Sigala.
5) Nsu kà nûm bò i – A fish bit his finger.

Underline the verbs in the sentences below.

1) Yǎ ba lǐn mà nèbti nji – My father makes gowns/clothes.
2) Luma nâŋ mbaŋ à fə'tì – Luma has cooked a delicious meal.
3) Mvɨ kà nûm bo Yeba – Yeba got bitten by a dog.

Exercise 13D: Grammar and Vocabulary with [ny]
Underline the nouns in the sentences below.

1) Nyùm tum mɨ – The sun is out/ The sun has risen.
2) Luma wê' nyùm ì – Luma is wearing her watch.
3) Bì to bà cha'ti Nyìkɔb – Come let's pray!

Underline the verbs in the sentences below.

1) Chi nyɨm mɨ majǐ nchì – The salt has melted in water.
2) Dɔb nyɨ̌' mɨ mvɨ lɛ – Dob has sent away the dog.
3) Mon nyɨ̌ mɨ ma kun – The baby as pooped on the bed.

Exercise 13E: Spelling and Tones
Circle the misspelled words or those whose tones have not been properly marked. Then write the correct word on the line provided.

1) Na nyɔ nyu ma ŋgwɛn – Mother killed a snake in the farm.

....

....

2) Nà'bila nǎŋ mbâŋ ŋgɔb – Nahbila cooked a pot of chicken.

....

....

3) Nyum kà ta nìŋkù' tìtì – It was   too sunny yesterday.

....

....

4) Nyìkɔb kà nebti nìndəŋ boà nsi – God made Heaven and earth.

....

....

Chapter Glossary

	Noun	**Verb**
[N]	Nă – mother Ni – elder/older brother/ also an honorific as in Mr. Nsu – fish Njì – hunger Nji –clothes/dress Njàŋ – niddle Nindəŋ – Heaven	Nèbti– to fix/make Naŋ – to cook Num – to bite Na'ti – to show/to illustrate Nɨŋ – to put Na – to speak using proverbs Nŏŋ – to sleep (formal usage)
	Noun	**Verb**
[Ny]	Nyùm – sun, hour, watch Nyìkɔ̀b – God Nyàmbà'nì – horse Nyo – snake Nyŏmnyòm – worm Nyad –buffalo Nyàm – animal Nyin – one Nyɔ'– disease Nya' – eggplant	Nyàmti – to mix Nyɔŋ – suckle, kiss (also nyɔŋti, to suck) Nyŏ' – to kill, murder, terminate (such as a club or association) Nyɨ̆ŋ – to dance, to tread on, trample (Nyɨ̆ŋ bɛn – dance) Nyɨ̆m /Nyɨ̆m– to melt, dissolve, become damp Nyɨ̆' – to drive off, expel, make haste, hurry, run after Nyam – to be selfish Nyăb/nyăm – to mix. also mà nyàmti Nya'ti –to tiptoe Nyɨ̆' – to defecate

	Noun	Verb
[ŋ]	Ŋkan – monkey	Ŋwăd – draw (especially, liquid)
	Ŋu – moon, month	Ŋŏ' – pinch, nip, wink (also ŋɔ̀'ti)
	Ŋgàm – conversation, speech, discourse	Ŋa' also ŋa'a – to open
	Ŋgàn –crocodile	Ŋad – roll up, wrap up (also ŋati)
	Ŋgɔb – chicken	Ŋwăd – to scoop
	Ŋwà'nì – book	Ŋom – to bend
	Ŋkì' – woven basket	
	Ŋgɔ' – termite	
	Ŋkab – money	
	Ŋkɔ̀d – fight	
	Ŋku – corpse	
	Ŋkɨ – rope, cord	
	Ŋka' – fence	
	Ŋkè̄ – bachelor/spinster	
	Ŋkɔ̀ŋ – bullet	
	Ŋkù – slimy vegetable	
	Ŋku' – widow(er)	

NOTES

CHAPTER 14

L & W

In this chapter, we shall look at letters [l] and [w] which have the same pronunciation as in the English language. You would notice that Mungaka Native speakers commonly replace the letter or sound [r] in English words with [l]. For example, it is common to hear speakers refer to Robert as [Lɔbɔ̀d], rubber becomes [lɔbà].

Lesson 14A: Practice the sounds of Speech

Read out the words in the first column, followed by those in the second column; then read the words in pairs, contrasting the consonant sounds. Do same for the last two columns.

[L]	[W]
Lo	Wo
Li	wi
Lɔ'	Wɔ'
La'	Wa'
Lǎ	Wǎd
Ləm	wɔm
Lə'tì	Wɔmtì

Exercise 14B: Grammar and Vocabulary with [l]

Underline the nouns in the sentences below.

1) Bà ləm jam ma ŋgwɛn – There are so many bats in the farm.
2) Lilì bǎ num u, ù jaŋ – If a mosquito bites you, you will get sick.
3) L̀ŋ ti a bɵ̂ Jàlla – My name is Jalla.
4) Bòla lùm wɔm – Bola is 10 years old.

Underline the verbs in the sentences below:

1) Kenna lǐn mà fuŋ Mìŋgâkà – Kenna can read Mungaka.
2) Nǎ suŋ ŋgâ Bùma ləŋni mbaŋ lɛ – Mother asked Buma to rinse the pot.
3) Bola to lam fɔmmvi – Bola will get married tomorrow.
4) Lǎ bà' ghâ – Pass/com this way.

Exercise 14C: Grammar and Vocabulary with [w]
Underline the nouns in the sentences below.

1) Ven wo lɛ ma laŋnjù' mfa mɨ – Pick up the stone in the courtyard and give it to me.
2) Mɨ nì sibo wɔm – I have ten fingers.
3) Yǎ kǎ kà vî bon wɔm – My grandmother had ten children.
4) Dema sô wɔbtì nì bò i – Dema has a ring on his finger.

Underline the verbs in the sentences below.

1) Mbôŋgə wâd mbùm ì – Mbongə cut herself.
2) Fě kà wâd tɨ jòm lɛ – Feh felled the plum tree.
3) Lêna wâ' mvà' majǐ bɔ' – Lehna threw the rubbish into the pit.
4) Sigala wɔ̂' nchì (Also Sigalla nì ŋwɔ' nchì.) – Sigala swims in the water.
5) Bì to bà wê mâŋgɔb lɛ – Come let's catch the hen.

Exercise 14D: Spelling and Tones
Circle the misspelled words or those whose tones have not been properly marked. Then write the correct word on the line provided.

1) Làma lam Ba Lɔbɔd – Lema got married to Ba Robert.
   ....
   ....

2) Nɨŋ wɔbti nì bo i – Put a ring on her finger.
   ....
   ....

3) Mon ma ndùn lən – The baby is sitting on the chair.
   ....
   ....

4) Lili boà lǎm lǐn mà tǎ– Mosquitoes and bats can fly.
   ....
   ....

5) Wǐ Mfòn jam – The King has many wives.

....

....

Chapter Glossary

	Noun	Verb
[L]	Lilì – Mosquito Lɨŋ – name Lùm – year Lɨm – tongue Lèŋ – chair Lɔ' – spell, curse Ləm – bat Lə'tì (introductory dance by men about to fire guns)	Lǐn – to know Ləŋni – to rinse Lam – to marry Lǎm– to gossip, to crawl Ləm – to grind Lo – to rain Li – to sleep Lǎ – to pass La'– to spend a night somewhere, stay

	Noun	Verb
[W]	Wɔmtì– respect Wi – (plural of ŋgwi – wives of), e.g. the King's wives – wi mfòn) Wotita – grinding stone Wè – art, handcraft Wà – a species of tree Wɔbtì – ring Wo – stone Wɔm – ten	Wèti – to tremble, shake Wom – to garden (as in wom fà' – to make garden beds) Wŏb – to hang in, put in, embrace, hang over something Wɔmti – to honor Wŏŋ – to hire, call, enlist, recruit, levy Wɔ' – to swim Wa' – to throw Wăd – to cut

NOTES

CHAPTER 15

Y

The letter [y] is pronounced in the same fashion as in the English language. You would notice that no Mungaka word ends with letter [y]. Mungaka words with letter [y] either occur at the beginning or in the middle.

Lesson 15A: Practice the sound of Speech

Read out the words in the first column, then read the words in the second column; then read the words in pairs contrasting the vowel sounds.

[Y]	
Yù	Yà
Yǎ	Yě
Yîn	Yàb
Yi	Yî
Ya	Yə

Exercise 15B: Grammar and Vocabulary with [y]

Underline the nouns in the sentences below.

1) So bə̂ yumfà' – A hoe is a tool.
2) Nǎ jûn yumtasɨ̀' ì mfi mbə̀ Dɔb – Mother has bought a new toy for Dob.
3) Yumfǎ' Ba bubti mɨ – Father's tool is broken.

Underline the Interjections in the sentences below.

1) Yəkà, mon lɛ jì'ti tìtì – The kid is very smart.
2) Yekà, mfə' lɛ tǐn ghâ' tìtì – See, the cold here is severe/ it's really cold here.

3) Yɔ̀ motŏ nì mèn – This car is dirty

Underline the adverbs in the sentences below:

1) Ù lŏ' ya ɛ? – Where do you come from?
2) Ù ghɛ̀ ya ɛ? – Where are you going?
3) Billa ya ɛ? – Where is Billa?

Underline the verbs in the sentences below:

1) À bŏŋ mà yu'ni Ba boà Nǎ – It is good to obey your parents.
2) Yu' yum yì n-chu a – Listen to what I said
3) Yɔ̀ ŋgàŋ–ŋgam yəni– This soothsayer can foretell well.

Exercise 15C: Spelling and Tones

Circle the misspelled words or those whose tones have not been properly marked. Then write the correct word on the line provided.

1) Yùm mon və mɨ – The baby's stuff is missing.

....

2) Yekà, jì'ti bu' ù – Be careful!

....

3) Yî Ba bê̂ ŋgàŋ–ŋkàb – His father is a rich man.

....

4) To bà yè mŏ'yum – Come let us do something.

....

5) Yŏ mɨn lɛ nì màd mbɔ̀ŋkɛd – This person has a good character.

....

6) Yum yàb bə ya ɛ? Where is their stuff?

....

Exercise 15D: Write down five words that have the letter Y

1) ....
2) ....
3) ....
4) ....
5) ....

Chapter Glossary

	Noun	Verb	Pronoun	Interjection/Adverb
[Y]	Yum – thing, object; Plural –kě	Yə, also yəni– to look	Yɔ̀ – this (pronoun)	Yəkà – interjection – behold, take notice, take note.
	Yumfà' – tool, kěfà' (plural)	Yu' – to hear, listen	Yǎ – possessive pronoun – Singular – mine – normally precedes a noun).	Yâ – a manner of shaming someone
	Yumtasɨ̀' – toy, plaything; kětasɨ̀' (plural)	Yu'ni – to obey	Yù – yours	Ya – where, (normally followed by the interrogative particle, ε)
	Yumndab – furniture; kěndab (plural)	Yu'ti – to taste	Yǎ – mine	
		yě – to do, make	Yìn – yours (third person plural)	
			Yì– his/hers	
			Yà – my	
			Yàb – their	

NOTES

ANSWER KEY

1A: High Tone

Kaŋ, ten, bon, chu, chi, etc.

1B: Low Tone

Ntòn, ntò, chì, nyàm, kè, etc.

1C: Rising Tone

Kǎ, nǎ, dǒ, kě, tě, tǐ, tǒn, etc.
Kɔ̀b, nchù, nsɔ̀ŋ, etc.

1D: Falling Tones

1) Mômùnŋgwi (Mômìŋgwi), Mômumbaŋ, mômbi, etc,
2) Mânyàm, mâkaŋ, mâkɔb, mânsu, mândìkàŋ, mâmban, etc.
3) Ndâ-tìtà, ndâ-fù, ndâ-nyàm, mbâŋ-fù, mbâŋ-nyàm.

2C: Nouns

1) Mbàb, bàm
2) Bǎm, ndab
3) mbad

2C: Verbs

1) Nlad
2) Kab

3) Fa

2D: Nouns

1) Kè
2) Kè
3) Led
4) Led
5) Nswen, ited
6) Lela

2D: Verbs

1) Kê'
2) Nèbti
3) Lěd
4) Běd
5) Běd

2E: Spelling and Tones

1) Mbab (mbàb)
2) Bam (bàm)
3) Na (nǎ)
4) Na (nǎ)
5) Bed (běd)
6) Ke (kè)
7) Ke'fɨn (Kě'fɨn)
8) We' (wê')

3B: Nouns

1) Bɛn
2) Ŋgèn
3) Ŋgwɛn
4) Fèd

3B: Verbs

1) Bɛn
2) Kêd
3) Bɛti

3C: Nouns

1) Làŋ
2) Làŋ
3) Kə̀m
4) Njə̀mbi
5) Ləm

3C: Verbs

1) Nləm
2) Chêd
3) Kə
4) Chə̀lî
5) Kə̀lî

3D: Spelling and Tones

1) Kɛd (kĕd)
2) Mbikèd (mbikɛd)
3) Chə'tu (chə̆'tu)
4) Bɛd (bèd)
5) Fed (fɛd)
6) Kəm (kə̀m)

4B: Nouns

1) Lilì
2) Mì'
3) Njə̂mbî

4B: Verbs

1) Lĭn
2) Li
3) Fì'tî

4C: Nouns

1) Mvɨ
2) Lìŋ
3) Lìŋ
4) Lɨm

4C: Verbs

1) Kɨb
2) Fĭn
3) Kɨ:
4) Tɨ̂
5) Tɨ

4D: Spelling and Tones

1) Mà (ma)
2) Bə (bə̂)
3) Nchi (nchì)

5B: Nouns

1) So
2) Sogè
3) Sòŋkù

4) Bon

5B: Verbs

1) Kôm
2) Bom
3) No
4) To

5C: Nouns

1) Kɔ̀b
2) Fɔmmvi
3) Fɔmmvi
4) Bɔnì

5C: Verbs

1) Lɔ̌'
2) Lɔ̌'
3) Kɔ'
4) Bɔ̌ŋ

5D: Nouns/Pronouns

1) Ù
2) Ù
3) Tuŋ
4) Vu
5) Lùm, u
6) Tundab

5D: Verbs

1) Tum
2) Nûm
3) Jûn

5E: Spelling and Tones

1) Kɔŋ (kôŋ)
2) Ŋkò (ŋko)
3) Mbàŋ (mbaŋ)
4) Tuŋ (tùŋ)
5) Mɨ̀ (mɨ)

7B: Nouns

1) Pepè
2) Pəm

7B: Verbs

1) Pâd
2) Mpad
3) Pèti
4) Pèti
5) Mpǐ'

7C: Nouns

1) Bàm
2) Tab, ndab
3) Bàtì

7C: Verbs

1) Batî
2) Batî
3) Bati
4) Bàtî
5) Bèti
6) Bèti

7D: Spelling and Tones

1) Bamti (bamtî)
2) Bâmti (bamti)
3) Bùbti (bubti)
4) Mbàŋ (mban)
5) Mpaŋ (mpǎŋ)

8B: Nouns

1) Tâb
2) TV
3) Tita
4) Ŋgòndam

8B: Verbs

1) Ntaŋti
2) Ntasɨ'
3) Tànî
4) Nteti

8C: Nouns

1) Du'ti
2) Dù'tì
3) Du'ti

8C: Verbs

1) Du
2) Njɨ, du
3) Ta

8D: Spelling and Tones

1) Du (dù)
2) Dù' (du')

3) Na (nǎ) baŋ (mbaŋ)
4) Mɨn (mìn)

9B: Nouns

1) Kuŋ
2) Kûŋ
3) Kějɨ

9B: Verbs

1) Kêm
2) Kan
3) Kab
4) Kan

9C: Nouns

1) Gwè
2) Gàŋ
3) Gwǎnyìnyi
4) Gwè

9C: Verbs

1) Gâb
2) Gəbli

9E: Nouns & Adverbs

1) Bàghan
2) Ghə
3) Ghâ'
4) Ghâ'
5) Ghâ'

9F: Spelling and Tones

1) Gâ (ghâ)
2) Gha (ghâ)
3) Ghà (ghâ)
4) Gha (ghâ)
5) Ghè (ghě)
6) Ghə (ghě)
7) Kàb) (kâb)

10B: Nouns

1) Chi
2) Chi
3) Chèn
4) Chaŋ, mvɨ

10B: Verbs

1) Châb
2) Châb
3) Chăb
4) Chènti
5) Chènti
6) Chè'ni
7) Nchè'ni

10C: Nouns

1) Jaŋ
2) Jaŋ
3) Jaŋjaŋ
4) Jùŋ

10C: Verbs

1) Njə̂'
2) Njə̀'ti

3) Jun
4) Jŏb

10D: Spelling and Tones

1) Je'tì (jə̀'tì)
2) Chĭt (chĭd)
3) Jə'ti (jə̀'tì)
4) Chen (chèn)
5) Chenmu' (chěnmu')

11B: Adjectives

1) Fufu
2) Fɔm
3) Fɔm
4) Fə
5) Fə'ti

11B: Nouns

1) Făbsuŋ
2) Fà'
3) Fɨkəb
4) Fu'tu

11B: Verbs

1) Fa
2) Fûŋ
3) Mfûb

11C: Nouns

1) Vàvà
2) Vum
3) Vub
4) Vu
5) Vŭtu

11C: Verbs

1) Và'
2) Və'ti
3) Və'ti
4) Vi

11C: Adjectives

1) Vàgli
2) Vàglivaglì

11D: Spelling and Tones

1) fùŋ (fuŋ)
2) Fù' (fu')
3) Vùm (vum)
4) Vŭtù (vŭtu)

12B: Nouns

1) Mălàm
2) Mândìkàŋ
3) Mbà'
4) Mbǎ'
5) Mànjì
6) Mɨsɨŋ

12B: Verbs

1) Mmâ'
2) Mvî
3) Mǐ
4) Màŋni

12B: Adjective

1) Mĕn

12C: Nouns

1) Mfòn
2) Mfə'
3) Mbùm
4) Mfɨnyùm
5) Mbàb

12D: Nouns

1) Sàd
2) Săŋ
3) Sànjàb
4) Nsun
5) Sâ'nsi

12E: Nouns

1) So
2) Saŋ
3) Sòŋkŭ
4) Sogè

12E: Verbs

1) Nsâd
2) Sŭ'
3) Sĕ

12F: Spelling and Tones

1) Sìkù (sikù)
2) Sìbo (sibo)
3) Si (sì)

4) Mbaŋ (mbàŋ)
5) So (Sǒ)

13B: Nouns

1) Ŋkan
2) Ŋu
3) Ŋgàm
4) Ŋgàn

13B: Verbs

1) Ŋa
2) Ŋwà'ni
3) Ŋɔ̂'
4) Ŋatî

13C: Nouns

1) Njì
2) Nji
3) Nǎ
4) Ni
5) Nsu

13C: Verbs

1) Nèbti
2) Nâŋ
3) Nûm

13D: Nouns

1) Nyùm
2) Nyùm
3) Nyìkɔ̀b

13D: Verbs

1) Nyǐm
2) Nyî'
3) Nyǐ

13E: Spelling and Tones

1) Na (Nǎ)
2) Nǎŋ (nâŋ)
3) Nyum (nyùm)
4) Nebti (nèbti)

14B: Nouns

1) Ləm
2) Lilì
3) Lɨ̀ŋ
4) Lùm

14B: Verbs

1) Lǐn
2) Ləŋni
3) Lam
4) Lǎ

14C: Nouns

1) Wo
2) Wɔm
3) Wɔm
4) Wɔ̀bti

14C: Verbs

1) Wâd
2) Wâd

3) Wâ'
4) Wɔ̂'
5) Wê

14D: Spelling and Tones

1) Lam (lâm)
2) Wɔbti (wɔbtì)
3) Lən (lə̀ŋ)
4) Lili (lilì), lə̆m (ləm)
5) Wǐ (wî)

15B: Nouns

1) Yumfà'
2) Yumtasɨ̀'
3) Yumfà'

15B: Interjections

1) Yəkà
2) Yəkà
3) Yɔ̀

15B: Adverbs

1) Ya ɛ
2) Ya ɛ
3) Ya ɛ
4) Ya ɛ

15B: Verbs

1) Yu'ni
2) Yum
3) Yəni

15C: Spelling and Tones

1) Yùm (yum)
2) Yekà (yəkà)
3) Yǐ (Yǐ)
4) Yè (yê)
5) Yɔ̆ (Yɔ̀)
6) Yum (yùm), Yàb (yab)

A & E: Matching Pairs
Match the following words with their corresponding photos

Tà

Mbad

Kè

Pepè

ɛ & ɜ: Matching Pairs
Match the following words with their corresponding photos

Lὲŋ

Ŋgwɛd

Njὲmbi

Ŋgwɛn

I & Ɨ: Matching Pairs
Match the following words with their corresponding photos

Ghɨgha

Ghɨghàŋ

Lilì

Mândìkàŋ

O, Ɔ & U: Matching Pairs
Match the following words with their corresponding photos

Kù

Kɔ'tàŋ

Kɔ̀b

So

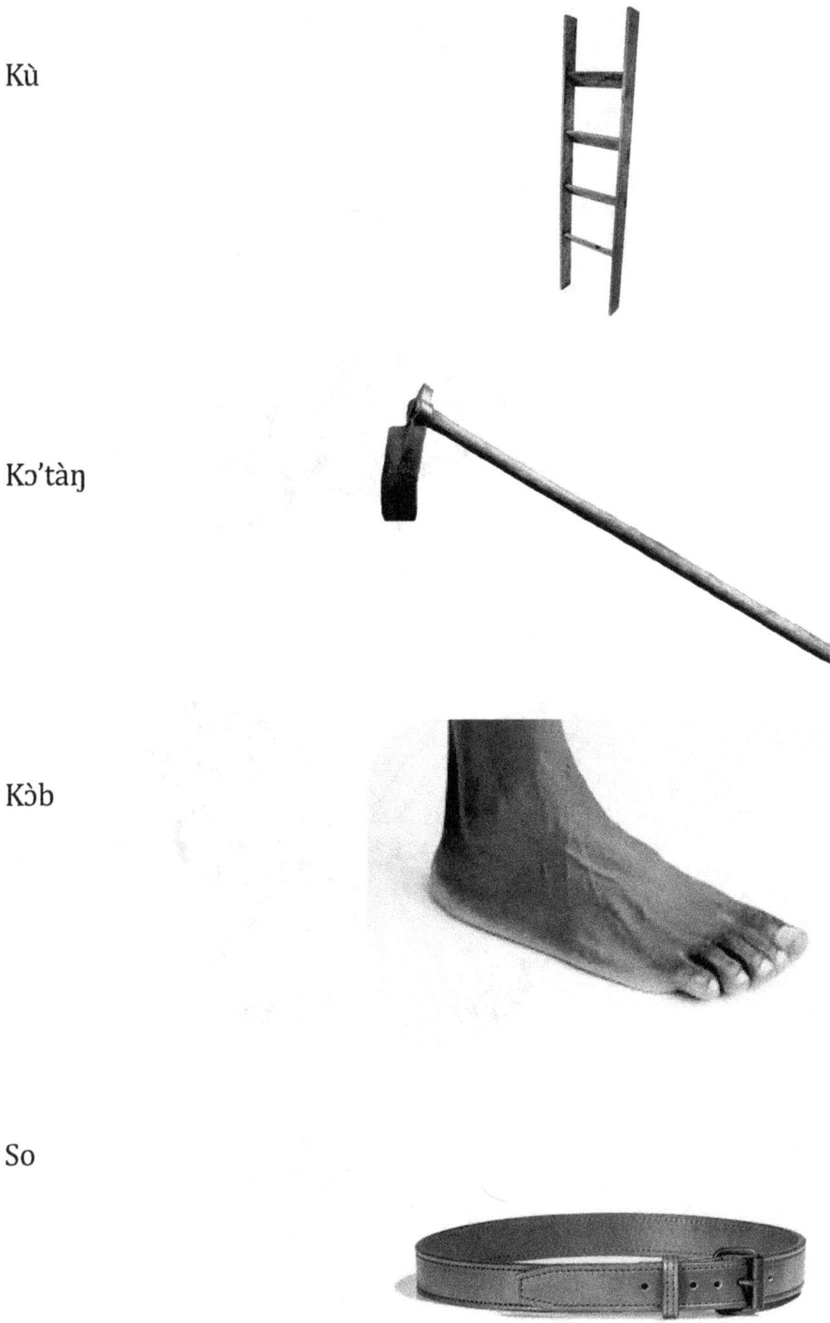

P & B: Matching Pairs
Match the following words with their corresponding photos

Bàm

Pàdŋkwèn

Bɔbŋgìŋ

Bon

T & D: Matching Pairs
Match the following words with their corresponding photos

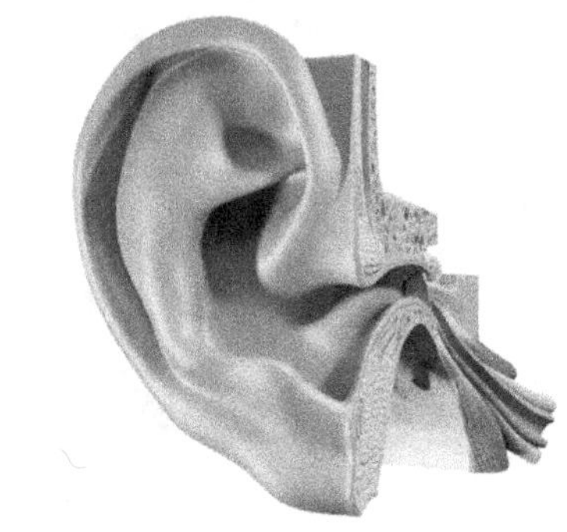

Dù

Tìd

Tuŋ

Dòg

K, G, & GH: Matching Pairs
Match the following words with their corresponding photos

Gàŋ

Kὲm

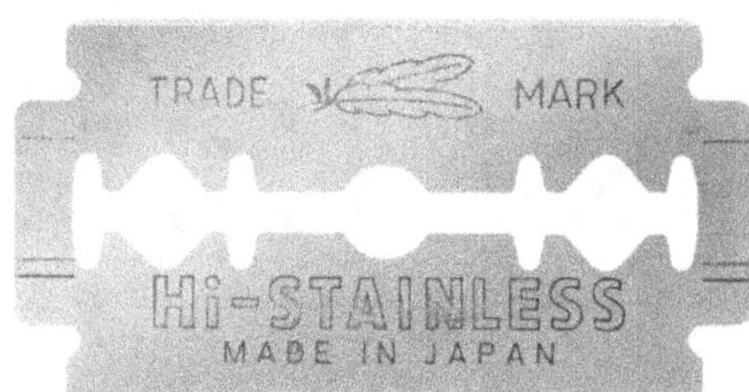

Gwǎnyìnyi

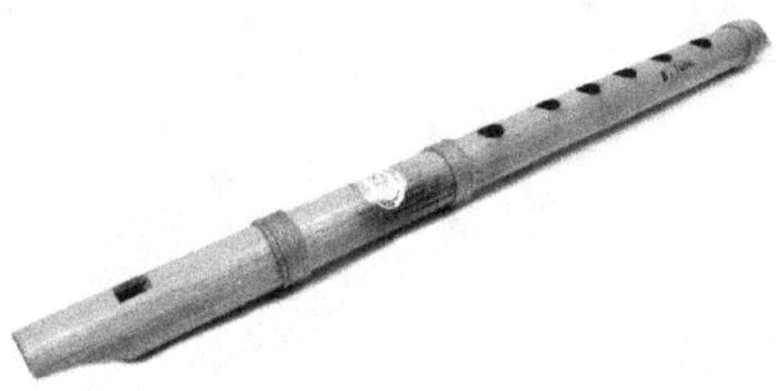

Ghan

CH & J: Matching Pairs
Match the following words with their corresponding photos

Chaŋ

Chěnmu'

Jɔŋ

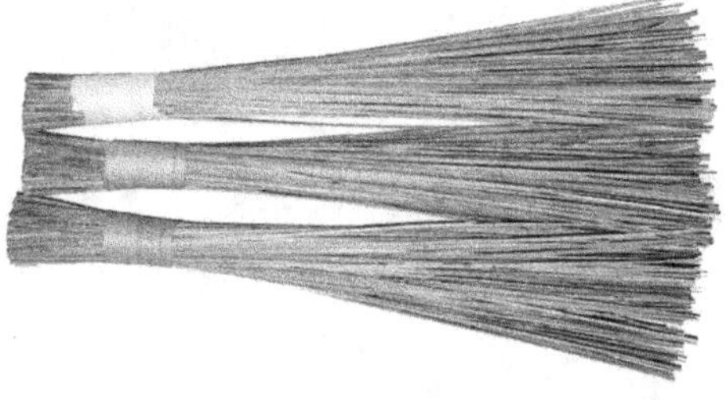

Jə̀tì

F & V: Matching Pairs
Match the following words with their corresponding photos

Fà'

Fɨkəb

Vàvà

Vaŋ

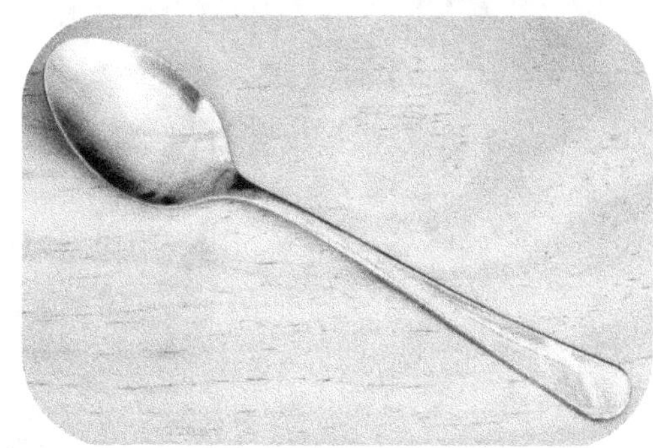

S & M: Matching Pairs
Match the following words with their corresponding photos

Sàd

Sikù

Mànjì

Mbaŋ

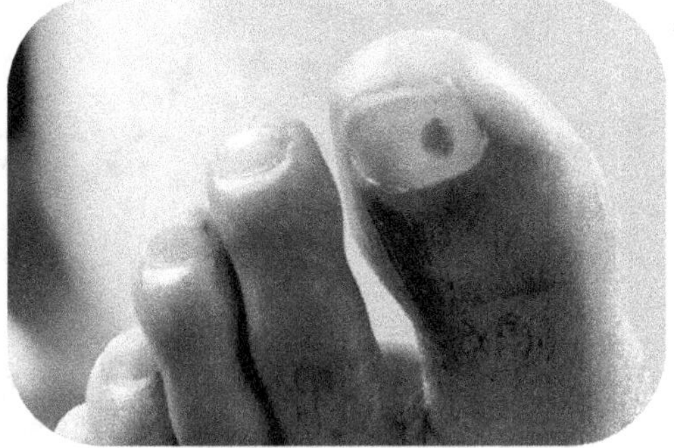

N, NY & ŋ: Matching Pairs
Match the following words with their corresponding photos

Nsu

Ŋkan

Nyàmbà'nì

ŋwà'nì

L & W: Matching Pairs
Match the following words with their corresponding photos

Lɨm

Lilì

Wɔbtì

Ləm

Old Vs New Vowels & Some Consonants in Mungaka (Mìŋgâkà)

Old (German) Alphabet	New (Cameroon) Alphabet
i	i
e	e
ạ	ɛ
a, ā, ą	a
ǫ	ɔ
o	o
ọ	ə
u	u
ụ, ụ̄	ɨ
ts	ch
dz	j
ɣ	gh
n	n
ń	ny
ṅ	ŋ